GUNNER SUBALTERN

GUNNER
SUBALTERN

Letters written by a young man to his
father during the Great War

by

JULIAN TYNDALE-BISCOE

LEO COOPER · LONDON

FIRST PUBLISHED IN GREAT BRITAIN, 1971
BY LEO COOPER LTD
196 SHAFTESBURY AVENUE,
LONDON WC 2H 8JL

© 1971 JULIAN TYNDALE-BISCOË

ISBN 0 85052 094 0

PRINTED IN GREAT BRITAIN AT
THE COMPTON PRESS
SALISBURY

CONTENTS

ILLUSTRATIONS

MAPS

FOREWORD

by Brigadier P. W. Mead, C.B.E., *(Retired)*
Secretary of the Royal Artillery Institution

It was in May, 1966 that I had the opportunity to read Julian
Tyndale-Biscoe's account of his experiences in the First World
War. I recognised it as a document of the greatest value to
the historical section of this Institution, and received permission
to have it typed and lodged in the archives.

The account takes the form of letters, or extracts from
letters, written by the author to his father, from Aldershot
where his Royal Horse Artillery battery first formed and
trained, from the battlefields of Ypres and the Somme, where
he was seriously wounded, from hospital in England, from
Ireland and finally from Egypt and Palestine, where he ended
the war.

Because artillery has usually been a 'supporting arm' to
infantry, cavalry or tanks, it is an unfortunate fact that
comparatively few eye-witness accounts of gunner actions have
appeared in print. In the 1914-18 war the part played by the
artillery was enormous and without it no battle was possible.
From Julian Tyndale-Biscoe's letters the wartime picture of
an artillery battery emerges most sharply, a picture made up
not only of periods of violence, blood and death but of
contrasting periods 'at rest' or on home leave.

This contemporary account of the battles of Ypres and the

Somme evokes by its very simplicity a measureless admiration for the stalwart courage of our countrymen of those times. ". . . We lost about a third of our men that day. It could have been much worse", wrote this young officer in the Ypres salient, and it is clear that no early relief was expected.

After he was wounded, and evacuated to England, his letters tell of incidents of lesser drama, but these incidents are still part of the picture of an army and a nation at war, and in the last seven chapters he moves to the Middle East, whose atmosphere is once again reflected most faithfully in the letters. The Gunner Subaltern was now an extremely active Intelligence Officer, equipped with a motor-cycle on which he strayed well beyond his forward troops, collecting a group of German and Turkish prisoners on his way back.

Gunners everywhere will be most pleased that Leo Cooper is to publish this manuscript; a far wider readership will find themselves transported most vividly into perhaps the most testing era of our history.
Woolwich

6 September, 1971   Peter Mead

EDITOR'S PREFACE

This book needs little introduction from the editor, but since the editor is also the author of the letters on which it is based, a little explanation is needed.

The letters were written to my father during the First World War. They were found in a bag some fifty years later, and fifteen years after my father had died.

My father had been ordained as a priest in 1887, and in 1891 he was sent to Kashmir as a member of the C.M.S. He was made a Canon and served Kashmir until India was granted independence in 1947. He then retired and came to Rhodesia, where he died some eighteen months later.

My letters to him were those of a young subaltern, and some of them were written under very odd conditions. Sometimes I talked about friends and relations in whom the reader would have little interest; because of this I have edited the letters to provide a continuous narrative of a young man's war and give them a more general appeal. I hope they will awaken memories in the survivors of my generation who also took part in that conflict.

J. T.-B.

First Flush
August 1914 to June 1915

CHAPTER 1

Join Something

We were at the O.T.C. camp at Cannock Chase when war was declared. There was great excitement that evening when, to celebrate the occasion, a fight ensued between two schools in which everyone joined, until there was a mêlée of about a thousand of us. Some chaps got on the top of tents and threw water over the seething mass. Sentry boxes were pushed over, with the sentries inside. The guard turned out and after unfixing bayonets, charged the mob with their rifles, but they were soon thrown to the ground and parted from their rifles and hats. The buglers ran to the officers' mess, and, a moment later, out galloped the Adjutant in his swagger mess uniform. He shouted out, 'Gentlemen, this is disgwaceful. Get back to your lines.' We were so surprised at being called gentlemen—we had never been addressed like this before—and because we admired him as a fine soldier, we all strolled back as if nothing had happened. Dear old Daddy Warner, our O.C., gave us a pi-jaw trusting that none of us had been mixed up in this affair. I had a swollen eye which must have made me suspect, but had got that in a boxing match the evening before.

The next day the regular battalion with which we were brigaded, marched off for their depôt, and we had to hand over half our tents which were wanted by the Army. This meant doubling up, with sixteen to a tent, and, of course, we could not sleep much. We amused ourselves by sallying forth and making sudden rushes at a number of tents, running up to the top and sliding down amidst volleys of oaths from those inside. Each time a sentry approached, we scuttled back to our tent causing, of course, an awful jam at the entrance.

The following day, camp broke up, and we went our different ways. Arthur Hamilton and I had proposed to go on a cycling trip, but decided to try to join some regiment instead. I wired to Cousin Victor [commanding King Edward's Horse] to ask if I could enlist in his regiment. He replied, 'Regiment full strength—join something.' Arthur was lucky, and has been accepted for the Sherwood Foresters.

The next morning I saw an advert in the paper that Kitchener wanted 2,000 officers, so rushed off to the Barracks at Bedford and Hertford, but without result.

On Tuesday I went to see Uncle Albert commanding a reserve brigade, R.F.A., at Woolwich. He suggested that I should put in for the Shop where he said his son, Norman, was going and where the course had been reduced to six months. I thought that much too long because the war would probably be over by then. It was all right for Norman, as he was only sixteen. He, then, kindly gave me a letter to Major Dooner at the War Office. So I went there straight away and was finally ushered in.

He asked me what school I was at, and when I told him [Trent College] he said: 'Oh! I inspected your Corps last June.'

'Good Lord, Sir! So you did,' I replied, and felt a fool for not having recognized him at once, especially as I was one of those who had been called out to command the Company on field manoeuvres.

From a remark he made, he evidently thought pretty highly of our Corps.

He then asked me my rank and other questions. When he learnt that I had Certificate A and was in the shooting eight, etc., he gave a grunt and told me he would arrange for my name to be gazetted during the next week or so.

I scanned the papers eagerly. Meanwhile, I ordered my uniform. When cycling back from London to Harpenden, I met convoy after convoy of private cars of all kinds travelling south as hard as they could go. Each car carried a placard in front with the letters **W.D.**, which I suppose stands for War Department.

It was not until the 12 September that I was gazetted, and my papers arrived that morning instructing me to report immediately to C Battery, R.H.A., in Aldershot.

As my uniform was not ready, I went off in my O.T.C. uniform with makeshift alterations on the sleeve; I was in great glee about being posted to the R.H.A., having visions of galloping about with a fully trained battery.

Who should I bump into on Waterloo Station but Uncle Julian, all dressed up in gold braid, etc., on his way to take charge of remounts in France. We travelled together as far as Aldershot, where I got off. He said I was jolly lucky to have got such an appointment. When I reported, however, they knew nothing about me, and told me to go to Deepcut which was my probable destination.

On reaching Deepcut, I found a camp of wooden huts, and with some trepidation entered the officers' mess—a place I had always regarded as the holy of holies. There, I ran into a kindly old major who told me what I had to do about reporting, etc. Later, I was taken by the Adjutant to my Battery Commander, Major Hawkshaw—a bald headed old man with a fringe of white hair, who gasped and sighed and told me to come along with him to the Battery.

Where were the guns and horses? All I could see was a large crowd of men in their civilian clothes marching unendingly to the voice of various sergeants, on a large gravel square, much to the detriment of their boots. The Major said, 'Here is the Battery—I would like you to train these men.' When I told him that I had had no artillery training, he said, 'Oh, that does not matter, you just watch the others do it, and then do it yourself.'

After a few more sighs, he said he would introduce me to Roberts, the other subaltern. Roberts had a glaring eye and was immaculately dressed; he had just been lecturing the men. He struck me as frightfully efficient, and I soon learnt that he had just left the Shop after two years' training. I could see he thought me quite useless, which, of course, I was.

On return to my quarters, a man reported himself to me saying he was my batman. As I am used to shifting for myself, I could not see that he would have much to do. On my going outside, however, to a nearby tap to collect some water for a wash, he rushed over and took the bucket from me—my first lesson at being an 'orfficer'!

K Battery, R.H.A., shared our mess. There were about twenty of us in all. There was another fellow called Paul who was in the same predicament as me. He had just left Harrow.

After spending three or four miserable days there watching the men being marched everlastingly round the square, feeling as sorry for them as I was for myself, I again broached the subject to the Major about getting some training. He thought it unnecessary, but finally agreed to ask the Colonel. I hear that my Major retired from the Army *before* the Boer War! After a week, orders came for my posting and I was ordered to Woolwich for training and hoped that I might find myself in Uncle Albert's Brigade.

On arrival at the R.A. Barracks, and just as I was putting down my bags in my room, bare except for a bedstead and a chair, who should come in but Uncle Albert himself, saying he thought it was I who was coming when he got the wire. I will never forget his kindness both then and when I had asked him before about getting a Commission. He took me round to the mess and gave me lunch, although I knew he was terribly busy. He introduced me to various young officers and to a funny little redfaced major whom I was to serve under, and when he left me he gave me half a sovereign. This has come in very handy because I have as yet received no pay.

Our pay is 5s. 7d. a day. This is 1d. more than the infantry, but will not go far as messing is 5s. 0d. a day. The outfit allowance, I am told, is £25—this should cover the cost of my uniform and sword which ought to arrive soon.

We have nearly completed our eight weeks' course here. It has been most interesting and pretty strenuous. Stables from 6 to 7 a.m., then to the Shop from 8.30 to 1 for gun drill, ranging and lectures, etc., then from 2 to 5 with the battery for mounted and dismounted exercises, and, finally, riding school from 6 to 7 p.m. with Major O'Hearn, a prince of riding-masters. This was the greatest fun, but how stiff and sore we were at first! 'Drop your reins, cross your stirrups, fold your arms, ter-rot!' for nearly half the time, then over the jumps and sword-drill. His nonstop and colourful curses were a wonder to hear, but if he saw a flicker of a smile, he was on to us like a whiplash. He asked every newcomer whether he could ride. We had fortunately been advised to say no, but one newboy, just over from Canada, replied that he had been 'brought up in the saddle'.

'So you think you can ride,' said O'Hearn in an ominous voice. 'Take that horse over that jump.'

Just as it was clearing the jump, O'Hearn gave it a flick with his whip that made it give a queer twist of its hindquarters. When the Canadian picked himself up from the ground, O'Hearn merely remarked, 'I thought you said you could ride.'

The only time for mugging up our manuals and books on artillery and horsemanship, etc., had been after dinner at night. Some of them tended to send one to sleep. One of them contained pages and pages of definitions, with a long list of questions and answers at the end, on which we are examined from time to time. The questions must be answered as per handbook. One of the questions was 'Why has a gun wheels?' Now anyone who had not studied his handbook would probably answer 'To make it easier to pull', or 'To make it more mobile', and thus show his gross ignorance! The correct and only answer is, 'To overcome friction'!

One of the sergeant instructors caught us all out when he picked up a large spanner, saying, 'This is the McMahon spanner. Why is it called the McMahon spanner?' (This was not in the handbook.) Before we could think of an answer, he said, with a smug look on his face, 'Because it was invented by a Mr McMahon.'

We were a motley crew to start with on this course. Some had to be weeded out: they behaved badly when we were being drilled by N.C.O. instructors at the Shop and gave the whole squad a bad name. Uncle Albert had us all in and gave us a dressing down. More effective than any cursing, he just pointed out the meanness of causing annoyance to those who, at great extra trouble to themselves, were trying to teach us our job. He kindly let drop to me later that he had had excellent reports from the Commandant on several of us, which cheered me no end.

A few of us were picked out to take the rest at gun drill. This is always done at the double and we enjoyed making the others sweat, for a change. We became quite adept at giving the command 'Without drag ropes preee-prrdvnce', (which, of course, means 'prepare to advance'). The last half snapped out as one syllable and immediately followed with, 'As you were!' if the men were not off the mark like a shot from a gun.

The greatest fun has been the mounted exercises with the Battery. I had two nice chargers allotted to me, one, a black mare, was a beautiful jumper. When a captain was posted to our Battery and was inspecting the stables, he took a fancy to my mare and asked me whether she handled well, etc. In my innocence, I cracked her up. He then told me to have her sent round to his stables!

The first time I was detailed to take part in the ceremonial Church Parade at the head of the Brigade of some 500 men with the band playing 'Tipperary', as it invariably did on those parades, I felt a bit of a blood, all besworded and spurred, but also a bit scared that I should give the wrong order. We marched into the Garrison Church for the service.

One of my jobs was to pay the Battery. I had to collect over £500 in silver in two haversacks. The weight of it hanging from my shoulders rather unbalanced me and I staggered drunkenly to the hansom cab waiting outside and took it to my quarters, where I remained with it until pay parade at 2.30, thus missing my lunch.

I have met a lot of nice fellows here. Apart from Paul, there are two from Cambridge—one shared the same staircase at Jesus with Harold [his brother] and the other who is in my Battery stroked the third Trinity boat.

There is a tremendous crush in the mess. Five colonels, over a dozen majors and captains, and some thirty subalterns, the majority of whom are temporary, like myself. On my first night, I was initiated, as all newcomers are, by having to drink a glass of neat brandy during the hour we sit and chat after dinner. Oddly enough, it did not have any effect!

On mess nights, we sit at two long, beautifully polished tables—all the subalterns at one table. Everyone in mess kit, except for us temporary wallahs. The R.A. band plays light music and at the end, the Bandmaster marches up to take a glass of port with the President while the band plays 'Tipperary'. The Colonels take it in turn to be President. One night it was the turn of a very old colonel. When he gave the Royal Toast, he said: 'Gentlemen, the Queen.' (Shades of the Boer War!) There was a moment of dead silence, then everyone said 'The King', so all was well. Apart from the Toast, etc., we all stand while the National Anthems of France, Belgium and Russia are played.

A rather nice description of the gunner officers that is going the rounds is that the subaltern knows nothing and does everything, the captain knows everything and does nothing, the major knows everything and does everything, and the colonel knows nothing and does nothing! There is an element of truth in it, since we three subalterns are supposed to check every jot and tittle of our respective sections, consisting of two guns, the ammunition wagons, about fifty horses and all the harness, etc., and do all orderly duties, including inspecting the guards at night, in addition, of course, to being on all parades. Whereas the captain, apart from being responsible for the ammunition and wagon lines, seems to have a pretty easy time. The major, being responsible for every jot and tittle of the whole Battery and efficiency of every officer and man in it, and wishing to ensure that his battery is better than anyone else's, naturally does quite a lot, while the colonel, with four such battery commanders vying with each other, has only to ride round occasionally and nod approval.

The food here is gorgeous. For pudding we have ice cream handed round in the form of a huge cake. We can take nearly as much as we like, the only limitation being the fear of being thought greedy! I have put on over one stone since being here, a great change from the starvation diet we had at school.

CHAPTER 2

Godalming

Here I am in Godalming, living like a lord! By a stroke of luck, I managed to be billeted with Aunt Ethel and family, in her house which has stabling for my two chargers with rooms above for my batman and groom. Dorothy, Tom and Mollie are at home at present, and Tom has a little terrier called 'Ypres'. Jack is with his ship and Nata is nursing.

On leaving Woolwich at the end of November, I rejoined my Battery which was at North Camp in Aldershot. The men were in uniform and the Battery had two guns and some horses. The men seem a very nice lot on the whole.

The whole Brigade shared one mess. Another subaltern, named Lennox, had joined our Battery. He is a fourth year medical student. I shared a room with an American named Hughes. Old Major Hawkshaw was in good form and caused some amusement one evening in the mess while standing with his back to the fire and feet apart, chest out and a glass of sherry in his hand, by saying: 'I don't believe in all these angles and things, what I say is—"Gallop up to the top of the hill and poop off!"' We are likely to have a lively time in France if he takes us out!

The Brigade moved here from North Camp early this month. The Colonel arranged for a barrel of beer to be taken per Battery to fortify us on the march. On reaching the Hog's Back, a halt was called, and everyone refreshed himself.

We arrived about 4 p.m. and, with the rest of the Brigade, parked our guns in a huge shed near Farncombe. The horses are billeted all over the town. My horses are stabled at six different pubs. The men, of course, are billeted in scores of different houses. The day before we moved here, the Colonel had come himself to choose billets for the officers, and had arranged for three of us to go to a large house, belonging to Dr Collis Browne, on Holloway Hill, which was only 100 yards away from here! So it was quite easy to arrange the switch over. All the men are delighted with their billets and the inhabitants cannot do enough for them.

About a week after our arrival, a row which our Major had been having with the Colonel blew up, and he had to leave. We were sorry about this as he was rather a dear fellow—'A Bhoy of the Olden Times'. He may not have known much about modern gunnery, but he was a fine horsemaster. This just leaves us three subalterns to run the Battery. The whole thing is like a picnic—doing a little gun drill and riding about the country with the Battery on the pretence of doing field-work. It is great fun and the men enjoy it.

Around Christmas, the Battery was granted a week's leave in three batches. When Roberts was away and I was in command, an order came at 8.45 one morning, just as I was going down to give a lecture, that the General wanted all Battery Commanders with their full staff of signallers, etc., at Witley Station (4 miles off) by 9.30. It was a mad rush to change into riding kit and get the signallers to collect and saddle their horses. We trotted hard the whole way, arriving a quarter of an hour late. The General said he was angry because two batteries were late, adding, 'Generals do not like it', which amused us because he has only just been made one.

When my turn for leave came, I bought a second-hand motor bike for £25, tried it once and then went straight off to Holton on it, but had no time to get a licence. Near Oxford I was held up by the police and taken to the police station because, as it turned out, they were on the look-out for a spy reported to be riding a motor cycle. I was held for about two hours while they questioned me and rang up different places. Then the kindly sergeant said with a grin, 'You may go now, as you don't look like a spy—but get your licence when you get back.'

Just as I was going to bed shortly after my return, I received a message that a draft of horses for the Battery was due by train at Guildford at midnight, and had to be detrained and put into a train for Godalming. I jumped on my motor bike and headed for Guildford and found the train had not arrived. It was cold waiting. Fortunately, Hughes, the American, whom I had met at North Camp, turned up—he had been to a theatre—and said he would help me. At about 1.30, the train arrived with fifty-four horses. We worked hard with the aid of two porters who happened to be there. The boxes held nine horses each. As we removed the horses one by one, we had to use a shutter to keep the rest close to each other to prevent them kicking around and falling; we had to do the same in the other train. The horses were rather scared, so Hughes and I gave each one a heave with arms clasped behind its hindquarters. It took us four hours by the time we had fixed and watered them. We were covered with sweat by then. I gave Hughes a lift back on my motor bike. My light had blown out and as we had no matches we had to go very slowly with the dim light of a torch held by Hughes. We got back in time for a bath and change before first parade next morning!

Last Wednesday the whole Division was inspected by Lord Kitchener on a common about seven miles away. We started at 7.30 in a snowstorm. Our horses kept slipping and several fell. No one was allowed overcoats. Our hats looked like iced cakes. When we arrived, thousands of infantry were already forming up. Our four brigades of artillery formed up in front with us subalterns in front of our sections. There we sat with swords drawn for one and three-quarter hours. The snow melted down our necks into our breeches, and out of our knees. The horses got very cold. Mine was shivering so I kept banging my legs against his sides in an attempt to warm both him and my legs. At last, two cars swept past in front of us with Kitchener and company. They did not stop and the parade was over. We moved off, stiff with cold and rather deflated. We trotted hard all the way back, trusting to luck the horses would keep their feet. We got back at three, gave the horses a ten minute rub down, and then the men ran to their billets to change and returned to finish off the horses at 4.30. No man or horse was the worse for it, though we heard later that fifteen of the infantry had died of pneumonia. We received a general order yesterday congratulating the Division on its turn out and steadiness in the adverse conditions, and that it had made a favourable impression on some big pot of a French General whom Kitchener had brought to see the New Army in training.

Towards the end of January, Major Street took command of our Battery. He had recently been wounded while Brigade Major to the 1st Division, R.A. Things soon began to buzz. Parades started earlier, the Battery—all of us—having to double the two miles to the gun park. He gave lectures and made us give lectures. He took us out on intensive mounted drills, and generally stiffened up the training, and that was a tonic to us all. He has unfortunately now left to be Brigade Major to the 29th Division, R.A., after only three weeks with us. We are all sorry. A fine man and soldier, he taught us much during his short time with us, impressing on us that it was our duty to fit ourselves as quickly and thoroughly as possible to kill Germans.

I have started boxing among the men—there are some who have been professionals. One of them, Bombardier Sheward, who was middleweight champion of his county, a shy gentle fellow, is the instructor. We also go on cross-country runs. The other day we made up a Battery football team to play Charterhouse. They were too good for us as we had never played together before, but we certainly were nobly entertained by the boys. I enjoy taking the P.T., giving the men every sort of weird exercise. Last week we all hopped in time together, at double-knee-bend, down the main street.

Last week, just as I was about to fall in the Battery for the O.C.'s inspection, I saw smoke shooting up over Godalming, and shouted 'Follow me!' Off we went at the double to find the tannery ablaze. We were set to work chucking the leather out of the building. Among it was a lot of chamois leather, excellent for cleaning harness, so each man took unto himself a piece or two. At the end, when the Battery was forming up, I heard one of my sergeants asking a driver of his sub-section where his chamois leather was. When he said he had not got one, the sergeant shouted: 'Why not? Go and get a piece at once!'

I expected a reproof from the Major for cancelling the parade without permission, but he seemed pleased about it. The outcome of it all was a letter of thanks from the tannery-owners, enclosing £10 for our Battery funds. We did well out of that!

When the men of my section were marching across a field yesterday, they were singing, 'Who's your lady friend'. Just as the head of the column debouched on the main road, they came to the 'Hello', which they bellowed forth with great élan. A solitary cyclist happened to be passing by at that self-same moment and was so startled that he fell off, causing a whoop of laughter in which he was able to join after he had recovered from his fright.

A funny thing happened the other day. After a hard morning's outing, when I had just given the order, 'Battery prepare to dismount', down went my horse and started to roll. I nipped off and then, from my lowly position, completed the order: 'Dismount'. Much hilarity among the men.

We are to move in a few days for our final training at Aldershot and Salisbury Plain. It has been a wonderful three months here, having lovely rides all over the country with the Battery during the day and coming back to such a lovely and delightful home in the evenings. Locke, my batman, has made himself useful about the house. Always cheery and nothing too much trouble. He is obviously much attracted to the pretty maid who works here! There will be many sad hearts, I expect, when we leave. The townsfolk have been awfully kind to all the chaps billeted on them, and have treated them as part of the family.

My two chargers have been a source of unending delight. The bay has been a trap pony and is full of beans. The other, a

Chestnut named Warrior, is highly temperamental; he looks like a wasp. For his size, 15.1, he is the fastest animal I have come across and certainly much the fastest horse in the Battery over a short distance. He is a bit of a terror to my groom. The two animals are the greatest of friends. My groom was Second Whip to the Devon and Somerset—a splendid little fellow who keeps both the horses and harness in splendid condition except that Warrior is far too excitable to put on flesh.

A week after Major Street left, Major Erskine arrived. He had come from an R.H.A. Brigade in India. He is a tall, dark man, with a natty moustache. He has knocked off the morning runs and also the subalterns' lectures. The last is a pity because we had to mug up these lectures beforehand and had thus learnt a lot ourselves. [He became Equerry to the King after the War and was knighted.]

Our C.R.A., old General Princep, came to one of our Brigade field days, and galloped about shouting, 'Damn your eyes!' to all and sundry. He rode up to our Colonel who has a large nose (it was a cold morning) and said loudly in front of us all: 'Wipe your nose, Colonel!'

A few days later, we went on a four-day Brigade exercise. On the first night, we reached a village where we were to billet. We had been on the go for fourteen hours. After seeing to the watering and feeding of the horses and to the feeding and billeting of the men, we had a bite ourselves. It was after eleven before we were free to go to our billets. Roberts and I shared a comfortable room and, after glorious hot baths, we got into our beds for a blissful night's sleep—when the trumpets blared out a bally call to arms. With curses and groans, we tumbled out of our beds, climbed into our accoutrements and dashed out into the cold darkness. By the time we reached the lines, the men were already converging from their billets at the double. Lanterns were being lit and harness sorted out. Soon the horses were harnessed up and the teams hooked to the guns and limbers, and we all formed up in Brigade order, waiting expectantly for the next order—which was, 'Dismiss!' We were told that it was just a test alarm, but were given a pat on the back for the speed and efficiency with which it was carried out.

On the following day, we had a field-day, when we were supposed to be engaging the enemy in some rather open country. After our Battery had been in action (with blank ammunition) for a while, we were ordered to move to a flank by sections. I took my section some way to the rear before moving to the flank, and coming into action again. While Lennox happened to take his section more or less straight across. During most of this exercise, the Major was in great voice, and, when we were drawn up after the show to hear of our misdeeds, he let fly at Lennox. There they were, standing facing each other in front of the whole Battery, with the Major dressing him down for moving his section across in sight of the enemy. Lennox, not having been through the same sort of mill as we had at Woolwich (he had been with the artillery wing of the Edinburgh University O.T.C.), made the dire mistake of replying, saying that he considered his section was well covered by a ridge. Whereupon the Major simply chewed him up. It really was quite a comical spectacle. Of course, it is all in the game in artillery training, and helps to liven things up, and it keeps one on one's toes.

Last week I was ordered to attend a three-day air co-operation course at the Royal Flying School at Farnborough, so off I went on my motor bike. The class consisted of eleven majors and captains and eight subalterns. Work consisted of standing by tables with all sorts of instruments and measuring angles to aeroplanes. Two machines and observers were put at our disposal and they signalled to us by wireless and electric lamps. On the last day anyone who liked could go for a joyride. The plane I went in was a Vickers Biplane. The pilot helped me into a little seat in front and then got up behind me. The propeller, of course, was behind both of us. When I took hold of the sides, the pilot told me my hands would get very cold, but I replied, 'Never mind—I feel safer like this!' We went up 2,500 feet. It was glorious. There was a terrific wind, but we seemed to be hardly moving. The country looked like a picture postcard. I tried to talk to the pilot and shouted as hard as I could, but the wind was too strong. I could not even hear myself shouting. The pilot had some difficulty in landing, and had three shots. When he did land, the plane went rushing on, and I thought we were about to crash into a fire hydrant when fortunately a wheel came off which slewed us round.

One of the subalterns on the course was a great big hearty chap who had been in the Coldstream Guards, but had had to leave for some reason or other. When war broke out, he managed to join up in the Gunners, like the rest of us. His name, very appropriately, is Gunning—a very likeable fellow.

CHAPTER 3

Aldershot

We have been at Aldershot about a fortnight, and are off next week to Salisbury Plain for firing practice with live shells, etc. The place is crammed with troops of the New Army—only a few besides our Division have khaki. The rest wear a curious blue, of which, apparently, the War Office must have large supplies.

Three of our Brigades have been crammed into the R.A. Barracks, taken over from the 9th Division which had left the stables in an Augean mess. It took us days carting out the dung and making things shipshape. Large numbers of temporary wooden stables have been erected, in some of which our horses are quartered.

We have all our guns now and equipment has been pouring in. The last draft of horses arrived last week. Lennox and I took turns in choosing them for our own sections as they circled round us. We were sent a batch of drivers, mostly miners from the Midlands, whose only experience of horses has been the pit ponies. It is hard work training them in the short time before us.

Our old Colonel has been replaced by Colonel Browell, such a nice fellow whom we all hope will take the Brigade out to France.

Everyone was inoculated against typhoid—or nearly everyone—because some, to show their independence, refused, in spite of hard words from us and their N.C.O.s. We lined up in queues for it. The needle looked rusty and certainly felt blunt.

I ran a temperature the following day and, because of the glands under my armpit beginning to swell, the Major kindly suggested that I should go off to Godalming to be seen by the family doctor. I went off on my motor bike. Another subaltern in the Brigade, named Wellesley, was also running a temperature, so I persuaded him to come with me (he is related in some way to the Duke of Wellington). Next day my temperature had risen to 105°. The Doctor saw me and when he came again he told me I had blood poisoning and was lucky not to have lost my arm. He thought at first that he could not save it. After three days' pleasant rest, I returned to Aldershot.

The work here has been rather monotonous—parades all day from 6 a.m. until 5.30 p.m. and going round the guards every other night. I am sharing an empty room with Dobbie [became Governor of Malta]—an extremely nice fellow except that he talks of nothing else but horses. The men have horrid quarters.

We are all looking forward to moving off soon to practice camp. The change will do the men a lot of good. They have been getting sick of it here, and an increasing number have been coming up before the O.C. for various 'crimes'. I have naturally to be present when any of my men are on the mat. The *modus operandi* rather surprised me. The Major listens quietly at first, and then his countenance suddenly changes to one of great ferocity and he barks out: 'Take three days' pay,' (or four days', as the case may be). It seemed at first sight that evidently crime pays! But by the look on the culprits' faces as they are marched out, they appear to be well aware that they must expect a curtailment of their intake of beer during the following week.

We had a change from the daily routine when all subalterns were ordered to attend at the officers' mess to hear a lecture by the C.R.A. on military law. All he did, in fact, was read to us from the Army Act a list of all the crimes we could commit when we went on active service. It sounded like a sort of dirge with each verse beginning with the words 'While on active service', and ending with the refrain, 'Maximum punishment death'. After several such verses, we began to join in the refrain

—very *sotto voce,* of course—but were caught out occasionally where 'death' had been replaced by a mere 'seven years' hard labour'. It was a pleasant entertainment, followed by a social interlude with glasses of marsala.

We have now returned from an exhilarating practice camp on Salisbury Plain.

Each Battery marched there separately. The weather was glorious and I cantered along over the downs from time to time, by way of a change. We all hooked up in a field the first evening, and, after settling the horses, sat down to eat. The men were all served and then the Major took his slice of bully and boiled potato. The Battery watched in silent surprise. Then Roberts took his—still silence. Then I took mine and made a face, whereupon a burst of laughter from the whole Battery. I suppose it was the first time they had seen officers eat army rations.

We took three leisurely days to reach the camp. A regular wooden city had been built, holding over a hundred thousand troops, divided into numbers of camps and very easy it was to lose one's way.

Two of our Brigades were camped together in one enormous field. The officers had canvas huts in which we slept three to a hut on wooden floors. Parades started at 5.30 a.m. and lasted all day. A high wind blew almost incessantly while we were there. Everyone was very much on his toes as this was our test, with a lot of generals and highbrows about, which was manifest in furious gallopings and much swearing. On the first day, it devolved on me as Battery leader to bring the Battery into action. My insides felt like water as we approached an agglomeration of high-powered staff from the War Office, looking like gilded vultures awaiting their prey! All went off well, and each of us subalterns was hauled out in turn to engage various targets, being allowed ten rounds of live shell each.

When my turn came and the first shot had burst beyond the target, I was about to give the usual correction when old General Princep, who was standing by, said 'Drop a hundred yards'. I knew this was not as per drill book, but felt it wise to comply. At the end, the chief vulture gave me a warm pat on the back for everything else, but picked on this mistake. Princep very sportingly said it was his fault as he had told me to do it.

We heard that evening that C Battery of the next Brigade had been given a place called Old Cot Farm as their target, and they brought their guns to bear on Cot Farm which they saw on the map. They hit it first shot, but in it were all the range officers who were there to observe the fire. No one was hurt, but they rushed out like bees.

We had several days such as this, sometimes being cursed and sometimes commended. There was also a bevy of officers from a junior division who had been sent to watch and gain tips from us.

Everything passed off very satisfactorily and we were highly commended on our shooting, in spite of (or perhaps because of!) the Cot Farm incident.

On coming into action, the next Battery to ours got itself into a frightful mess. It all started by a horse getting its leg over a trace at a critical moment. The Battery Commander, instead of throwing an apoplectic fit, just sat back on his horse and roared with laughter—sensible fellow!

In these exercises, if some incident like this happens, curses generally start from the top downwards. The O.C. calls out the subaltern in whose section the fault has occurred, and dresses him down in front of the Battery; the subaltern then gallops back swearing blue murder at the sergeant of the sub-section concerned, and he passes it on with interest to the bombardier in charge who finally hands it to the driver, whose fault it might or might not have been. He, poor chap, can only curse his horse!

We had some glorious gallops across the Plain and visited Stonehenge. I, on Warrior, used to race Lennox on a huge steeplechaser of nearly seventeen hands, and always won over short distances. Warrior went like an arrow and I seemed to float somewhere over his withers. I lent him to another subaltern.

After about half a mile, Warrior deposited him in a ditch—and trotted home.

We returned by train: half a Battery to a train at half-hourly intervals. Our half-Battery entrained in thirteen minutes from arrival at the station to all on board—guns, wagons and sixty horses complete. When the horses were fixed, we manhandled the train forward to bring the rear portion alongside, so as to load the guns and wagons and jump on board ourselves.

The mess here has livened up a lot since we returned. We have got to know each other much better during the practice camp, and the officers of our Brigade, under the benevolent influence of our Colonel, are a happy if rowdy family, but champing at the delay over getting off.

Rumours, however, about leaving any day now are rife. An indication was the collecting of all our swords for sharpening! They have come back almost razor sharp.

We are drawing our mobilization stores, including casualty returns, field dressings and identity discs. They all help to keep up the interest. An order came round that those wishing to make their wills should do so now. On the other hand, there are field-days, etc., down in orders for many days ahead.

Hooray! We are off at last. Last night while we were dining at the mess, an orderly brought a letter to the president. When he had read it he said, 'Gentlemen, orders have come that the Brigade will be ready to move at six hours' notice.' This was greeted with a thumping of glasses, followed by a silence. Then we drank the health of all we could think of, including, of course, 'Sweethearts and Wives'. There were thirteen at mess that night, and I was first to get up!

Yesterday I was watching two of our rifle battalions [The 60th Rifles and Rifle Brigade] marching off all kitted up, as they passed my stables. They were singing lustily 'Are we down-hearted, No, No, No' to the tune of 'Son of my soul'. It made me feel suddenly sad, wondering how many of them would be alive in a month or so. Then I caught sight of Cousin Harry [Master at Winchester] marching with his men. He was heavily loaded up with a pack, etc., so I crept up behind him and attacked him from the rear. He was in fine fettle, and responded vigorously.

About ten days ago we had a most exciting time at the rifle range. Most of the men had never seen a rifle. When we got to the range, it was quite chaotic. No one seemed to know what to do. Men started to fire before orders were given and were not particular as to what they fired at. Some bullets hit the ground a yard or two off and whizzed off with a whine, while many more cleared the butts completely. Different people were shouting different orders, and, then, some soldiers from another division started walking along the butts in front of the targets! This resulted in yells of 'Cease fire!' from behind us, which seemed to have little effect. I do not think many knew what the sights of their rifles were for. Anyway, from a safety point of view, it did not appear to matter much where one happened to be in this fireworks display. I did not hear of any casualties, and the Brigade marched back in great good humour.

CHAPTER 4

To the Front

Here we are, somewhere in France, after countless delays. When we did get started, things went with a rush. There were eighty-five special trains which came into the station one after the other in quick succession, and we boarded half a battery to a train; we had an allowance of fifteen minutes to get on. I suppose the Infantry went off in half battalions at about five-minute intervals. Our half-Battery did it in eleven and a half minutes, which I think must be a record. I nearly ended my days while watching the headropes of my horses being fastened properly. I was standing between the next pair of rails on the far side from the platform, when an express whizzed upon me. I noticed it at the last second, and jumped like a cat, escaping by inches. It certainly was a case of 'the quick and the dead'.

The Major and Lennox had gone with the first half of the Battery. Roberts and I were left with the second half. A lady friend came to see Roberts off and all the men were agog, sticking their heads out to see him kiss her goodbye. Much to their disappointment, this did not happen!

On arrival at Southampton, we met the Major, who was in a hurry because the Battery had to be on board in double quick time. After a terrific bustle, detraining, getting the horses up the ramps and slinging the guns, etc., we got everything on board. Our Brigade filled two ships which carried about 300 horses and men and 50 vehicles in each.

We moved off at 4 p.m. and anchored in the Solent. I was officer of the watch from 8 to midnight, and had a lot to do finding out the different guards and seeing that all the horses were fixed up properly. After knocking up my relief, I lay down, dirty as I was, till 5.30 for stables at 6, not having undressed or had a chance of a wash. We remained in the Solent until 4 p.m. the next day, so in the morning, boats were lowered and we had boat races. Two of our subalterns had been lieutenants in the Navy about five years ago and were to the fore in these sports. We also raced a crew of seamen. In the afternoon, we had boxing tournaments which were first rate. We moved off and picked up our escorts of two destroyers at the old fort at Spithead. I took out my old telescope and had a last look at Hayling Island and saw Winhurst and the Crescent and our bathing box there in all its glory.

The ship rolled a bit and the guard made vain efforts at walking straight, but failed miserably. I was on duty the next night, too, from 12 to 4, and ordered the Chief Engineer to put out his cigarette, asking him what he meant by it. He seemed rather annoyed. We reached port about one and a half hours after my watch ended, and I was suitably greeted by Wellesley with *'Bonjour!'* We disembarked at 7 a.m. and had a terrific scramble getting the horses down the ramps. Then we marched off to a camp a few miles off and took the horses into a field full of long luscious grass, and let them loose. They kicked up their heels and went nearly mad with delight after their uncomfortable journey.

After stables that evening, the men played mouth organs and we had a sing-song until 10 p.m., when we saddled up and moved off. The roads were cobbled and slippery after the rain, and several horses fell. On reaching the station, which was lit with huge flares, we set to work entraining. We had to struggle with terrified horses, pushing them up ramps and forcing them into trucks marked *'40 hommes ou 8 chevaux'*. They had to be fitted endways—four at each end with their heads to the centre. It was a tight fit and a hard job forcing the fourth animal backwards into position. As there were only two ramps at our disposal, it was not until 3 a.m. that the Battery was finally

aboard—the men, of course, forty to a truck; the officers in first
class compartments. We rested most of that day while the train
crawled on, stopping every three or four hours so that we could
water the horses. Many French people came and cheered us,
and we made attempts to talk with them during the halts.
Several times the train started while we were off it, and we
had to run for it. We finally detrained at 11 p.m. the following
night and marched off two hours later. After a few hours in
the darkness one of my teams fell into a deep ditch—six horses,
wagon and all. It took us a whole hour to get them out. Two of
the horses, all mixed up with the traces and upside down, were
in a fury of excitement. We got the wagon away after removing
the ammunition and managed to heave one of the horses up
with the aid of a rope round its neck. We tried to do the same
with the other, but it made no effort to help itself and merely
groaned. We poured a bucket of water over it to startle it. It
lashed out with its forelegs but its hind ones did not move. As
it must have broken its back, the Major asked me for my
revolver. When he asked me if it was loaded and I had said,
'Yes', the horse at once jumped to its feet as perky as anything
with its ears cocked forward! This made us all laugh and we
resumed our march in a more cheerful mood.

We reached our billets on a farm at 5 a.m. and, after seeing
to the horses, we broke off for breakfast and a rest till eleven.
I fell asleep while eating breakfast. The officers are billeted in
the farmhouse, while the men have a barn to sleep in. Since
we shall all soon be in action together, I decided to share the
barn with my lot and told my batman that evening to put my
valise there on some straw. It turned out to be a rather verminous
place, so I moved outside and had a glorious sleep in the open.
At breakfast, Roberts told me that it was not *comme il faut* to
share quarters with the men. However, one of my sergeants—
Sergeant Yule—who was a farmer in Norfolk before joining
up, came to me with a long face saying there had been a theft
of a watch in his sub-section. I told him to fall his men in and
then gave them a pi-jaw about stealing from comrades when

we would all soon be in action together fighting Germans, etc., and said I felt sure that the watch would be put back again before stables that evening. At stables, Sergeant Yule came, beaming all over his round face, and reported that the watch had been returned, which, of course, cheered me quite a lot.

We can hear gunfire in the distance and expect to go up in a few days. It seems hardly true that after all the delays and disappointments we shall really be in it at last.

I lost my dear old horse Warrior on arrival in France. He got fever on board ship, and had to be cast. I have taken instead the spare horse to be my second horse. It is a most awful looking brute—more like a hippopotamus, and notorious for its cunning and viciousness. It is known throughout the Battery as 'Kaiser Bill'.

We are at last in what is commonly known as 'action'. At the end of May we moved up towards the firing line. Our Brigade went by one road in a column about a mile long. We passed some Indian cavalry. They looked a fine set of men with their beards and their lances—obviously very proud of themselves. We came to a place where there were signs of recent fighting and settled in a field. General Plumer came and inspected our lines: Kaiser Bill had a shot at kicking him! The next morning, we managed to get baths under a pump outside a farmhouse, much to the amusement of some French soldiers. One of them kindly chucked a bucket of water over me.

Later that morning, the Major told me to take the Battery trap and forage for bran and a pole for one of our wagons, as ours was broken. When I eventually found the A.S.C., they were loath to give me one, but when I pointed out that it was really their wagon, and we could not return it without a pole, they let me have one. The bran was harder to get. Fortunately I had taken a sack of oats with me and finally bartered it at a French steam mill. The Major was delighted with my spoils. In the afternoon I went off to find Arthur Hamilton whose regiment, I heard, was only five miles off. I caught a lorry going that way, but, on inquiring at Corps Headquarters, was told they had left. It was a rush getting back in time for stables, but I fortunately managed to pick up an R.F.C. car and the driver took me back at 40 m.p.h., for which I tipped him five francs.

Next day we continued our march to the front. Everyone was in great spirits. As we passed through a town [Bailleul] many of the troops who had been out in France for some time stopped to admire our horses which were in splendid condition. Our general turnout obviously made a big impression.

It was a dusty march and owing to a gas alarm we had to put on our ridiculous respirators, which looked like bits of damp stockings. Some ambulances of a Division [9th Division], which had preceded us by one week, came rushing by with wounded. This made us feel we were getting near a war. Finally, we arrived in the evening at the wagon lines of the regular Battery we were to relieve. They were in action about three miles further on. This Battery had been out several months, so their drivers at once began to fill up our men with a lot of hair-raising yarns. We spent the next few hours seeing to the horses and warning the men to keep a sharp watch on their harness, as the 'old soldiers' would probably try to relieve us of some of it.

Lennox's section was ordered to the front that night. Roberts and I took the rest of the Battery up the following night. We had orders to leave our swords at the farmhouse where we had been billeted. If we ever see them again, their only use will be to toast food. Going into action was a very tame affair. Half the night we spent in helping to remove the guns of the other Battery, putting ours in their places and training them on their targets—all by map of course. The dugouts are very comfortable. All is very quiet although we can hear quite heavy firing some miles to our flank [Ypres salient]. At present I am more comfortable, better fed and altogether enjoying life more than this time last year at school.

I enclose a few jottings made during the few weeks we were in action at Dickebush. It was really rather a tame affair on the

whole, but I suppose only meant to be an overture for beginners.
[They were as follows:]

We three subalterns take turn about at the O.P. [observation post], the trenches and Battery. My duties at the O.P. are usually from 5 to 8 a.m. and 1 to 5 p.m. From the O.P. we can see both our own and the enemy trenches very plainly. The Major likes to direct the firing himself from the O.P. We go down to the trenches to find out what targets the infantry want us to engage. After 'phoning' the Major accordingly, we report back how the shells are falling. We use our field telephones and our signallers are kept busy mending the lines as they get cut by bullets.

The trenches are about 150 yards from the Bosch. I was down the other day with my two signallers when we were asked to engage a ruined building some 50 yards behind the German trenches, which was a nest of snipers. We were to fire first with high explosive and then catch them on the run with shrapnel. The infantry were cleared out of the trench in front of the target from where we were watching. Soon the fun started. First a whizz, then a cloud of smoke with bricks hurled into the air and a roar; then the 'whishtbang' of our shrapnel. Soon the Bosch returned the compliment and started pelting us. We lay doggo. Most of their shells burst some 20 yards behind us, spraying us with earth and some bits of hot iron, but doing no damage. The heavy shells gave us some warning as they roared towards us, but the whizz-bangs startled us a bit.

While down there I saw a casualty for the first time. It made me feel sick. The man was being carried by on someone's back, bellowing like an ox. He had apparently been shot in the backside. What surprised me was a chap next to me saying with a grin, 'Lucky blighter'. That night we had our first casualty in the Brigade. A subaltern in B Battery had joined in a night raid with the Infantry and was killed. In Brigade orders next day, there was an order that artillery officers were on no account to join enterprises outside their proper duties without express sanction from the C.O.

One evening last week, being off duty, I thought of practising with my revolver as I am pretty hopeless with it. Nosing round a ruined house near by for a suitable target, I found a full-size head and shoulders picture of some saint or other, so without thinking I stuck it up against a bank and started blazing away. Just then a Padre came up and I gave him a cheery 'Good evening'. To my surprise he was very rude, and said it was a pity an Irish regiment had not passed by and shot me. This annoyed me and I am afraid I was rather short with him. It turned out that he was the R.C. Padre to the Division and he reported me to our C.R.A., General Princep, who is an Irishman. He told the Colonel to see me about it, who told the Major to see me about it, who told Roberts to see me about it, who did so, and I told him to shut up.

Old Princep came round two days later when I happened to be on duty with the guns. He was in very good form and his anger with me seemed to have evaporated.

I forget whether I have told you of the make-up of our Brigade. Among the officers, Colonel Browell, the Doc, and two subalterns, Cavanagh (Adjutant) and Parry (Orderly Officer) are at Headquarters. Each of the four Batteries has a captain or major as O.C. and three subalterns. At the Brigade ammunition column a Captain is in charge, and the Vet. Our Battery (like the others) has four guns, each in charge of a sergeant with five other ranks. There are six signallers of whom two are usually at the O.P. and two with the F.O.O. [Forward Observation Officer]. Then there are the batmen and cooks who are, of course, all trained gunners. There is also the Battery clerk and the fitter. The number actually at the guns is therefore only about thirty-five, who, with the four subalterns in forward areas represent about one-third of the Battery's strength. The three subalterns take it turn about to be either with the guns or at the O.P. or as F.O.O. with the infantry, while the O.C. is, of course, ubiquitous. The rest of the Battery, with the 120 horses and the wagons, is at the rear under the sergeant major. In peacetime, with a six-gun battery this is normally a Captain's command.

I met Cousin Harry on Saturday as I was going to the O.P. He came along, too, and I showed him what could be seen from there of his and the German trenches which interested him greatly. In return, he gave me a tin of tobacco which I gratefully accepted, as I had run out. That evening, I took a party of men to bathe in a brewery. Hot water was poured into a lot of old beer barrels.

A rat ran over my face last night in the dugout. I tried to shoot it with my revolver, but it ran into my trousers. When I shook it out it jumped into my boot and from there made its escape, to the relief of Lennox, who shared the dugout with me.

We were up all last night firing and are starting again in five minutes, so must stop.

We came out of action about a fortnight ago, after handing over to a battery of another division, and are billeted in a large farm where we have been polishing up our signalling and gun drill, etc. Last week we had some sports which were a great success. Apart from the usual races for an inter-sub-section challenge shield, we had boat races on wagon poles, six men on each running backwards astride the pole with a cox steering round buckets of water and between others down an incline. Several crews capsized. The old soldiers' race caused great excitement as the sergeant major and Q.M.S. came first in a dead heat. To my surprise I won the officers' race. That caused quite an uproar as there had been a lot of betting on it. I had not intended to enter for it, having a bad toe, but I found that both my sergeants had put money on me. The mounted tug-o'-war was great fun. The men, riding bareback, had to let go their horses' heads while hanging on like grim death to the rope with both hands. Some of the horses started walking off, leaving their riders suspended on the rope. Soon the rest were galloping all over the place, with the riders who still remained on vainly trying to hold them in check as they only had halters. There were six officers there—we three plus three from Brigade H.Q., including the interpreter (a Belgian and a delightful fellow). The grand finale was wrestling on horseback, bareback, of course.

Sub-section versus sub-section with teams often from each. There were some great fights—men locked in death grips, with their horses at full gallop. When the horses parted, down they would fall between. There was also an officers' contest. I escaped disaster when my opponent's horse and mine parted, by jumping on to the neck of my opponent's horse, and we fell together. Prize-giving took place after tea. Madam, the farmer's wife, presented the prizes. One of my sub-sections won the challenge shield which consisted of a bit of tin painted in gaudy colours!

We are hoping to be off soon to something more exciting. It is very hot here now, and water is becoming a serious problem. The horses are drinking up all the ponds and we have emptied the poor farmer's well.

Last Sunday a very nice chaplain gave us H.C. before breakfast and we had Church Parade later in a large field.

On Monday I had to attend a Field General Court Martial. The President was Captain Ling, whom I knew as he had been an instructor at the Shop. The other member was a first lieutenant. The prisoner was a sergeant who had been charged with hitting a military policeman. He seemed a decent sort of chap, and when the President asked him 'Guilty or not guilty?', he replied, 'Guilty sir'; I was struck with the fatherly way Captain Ling spoke to him, suggesting that he should plead 'Not guilty', so the facts of the case could be sorted out. It turned out that he and a few others had got tight and he lost control of himself when he was arrested. I, as junior member, had to say first what I thought the sentence should be, and thought it would be enough if he were reduced to the ranks. The others considered he should also be given Field Punishment No. 2 for thirty days. This means no cigarettes, plus extra fatigues, and is not as bad as F.P. No. 1 which includes being strapped to a gun wheel for an hour at a time. In any case, it [F.P. No. 2] hardly applies, except for no smokes, while at the front.

PART TWO

Ypres

July 1915 to February 1916

CHAPTER 5

Zillebeke

We have come into action again. This is the first bit of spare time I have had for three days. We moved off from our billets on Friday afternoon. As usual, one wagon managed to fall into a ditch. After several miles, we reached a town [Poperinghe] where we were stopped as lots of London buses filled with Tommies rolled by, giving a homely touch. It might have been a busy street in London except there were no advertisements adorning the buses. We reached our wagon lines at dusk, where we gave our horses and ourselves food and drink and started off again about 9 p.m. After a couple of hours, we marched in silence passing what looked like Tom's Dog [nickname for Ypres]. With all the crump holes about, it was difficult to drive. Our cook's cart capsized, but fortunately the food was undamaged. We reached our positions at about 1 a.m., and then had to work like niggers to get the horses away before light. It was like an obstacle race getting the guns up past dozens of crump holes with the aid of a dimmed torch in front of each team. One lot got a wheel caught by a ruined building making the horses mad with excitement; this delayed us a quarter of an hour. It was already getting light when the last four wagons came up, so we just unlimbered them and ran them into a hedge and sent the horses away. We put everything under cover during the next half hour, and were able to turn in until 6 a.m., we then set to dig ourselves in surreptitiously until nightfall, when we built parapets round our guns and roofs, to support two feet of earth on top for which we had to find timber.

There were two trees about a quarter of a mile in front of one of my guns which were in the line of fire. After setting tasks for everyone, I went off with two sergeants and two bombardiers, one of whom was Locke, my former batman. We had a bit of trouble at first, finding out which the two trees were, as things looked so different. Near by, there was a French gun all smashed to pieces and the dead horses smelt horribly, but we soon got used to it and started chopping. The axe was very blunt, and we took a long time, taking it in turns. The Germans started shelling the woods some 200 yards away, but did not bother us. The second tree was a great oak. When nearly ready, we used a rope to pull it, as we had to be careful of the way it fell to avoid damaging telephone lines and try to drop it over a place full of crump holes. As it started to fall we had to run like rabbits, hoping not to trip up. Sergeant Bliss, however, fell with the tree on top of him. We thought he was squashed, but luckily, he fell in a crump hole with the tree across it. The Major was passing with signallers at the time, and was rather concerned when he heard the tree fall and asked if anyone was hurt. We then went to forage for timber in a ruined farm, but did not find much. Just as we were leaving, Locke was shot in the thigh. He was in great pain, poor chap. I stopped a Tommy who was passing and got his field dressing. We carried Locke back to the Battery and then went on digging till dawn.

I heard from Harold [his brother] that he had got his Commission in the R.N.A.S. He told me his pay would be 14s. per day. I am actually getting 3d. more than this, made up in this way— 8s. 6d. a day pay, 2s. 6d. field allowance, 2s. 6d. lodging allowance and about 9d. a day officers' mess allowance to drink the King's health. I have just heard from Cox & Co, that I have a balance of £32 so told them to send £5 to my school appeal fund as they are apparently in a bad way with so many chaps joining up.

We are living in great style here with a telephone from the officers' dugout to the cook-house and to the signallers' dugout near the Battery. The other day we invited Parry and the Doctor from Brigade Headquarters to dinner. Just as I had gone to meet them and we were near the cook-house, the Germans suddenly opened on us with a salvo of H.E. Our wretched guests and I made a concerted dive into the cook-house dugout where we crouched in a somewhat undignified position while the ground rocked. I had to apologize to them for their warm reception.

There were some men in a ruined house about thirty yards from here when the Germans started crumping it, and they all ran out like rabbits. Wellesley, who had been watching the performance with me and had an eye to business, rushed into the deserted house and collected two nice chairs which seemed in good shape and carried them off in triumph to his dugout.

After another strafing, I found Sergeant Grant with a worried look, hunting about in a newly made shell hole about twenty yards in front of his gun. I asked him what was wrong. He said that his aiming post had disappeared, which made me laugh, as I knew how fussy he was about his equipment. He cheered up when I told him that I would see he got another.

We keep finding quite a lot of dead fish in our field. There is a small lake close by, and they must get blown out during shelling.

On the way to the O.P., we have to pass a place known as Suicide Corner which is subject to frequent bursts of shrapnel. After a dash along there, one continues in a trench which is even more of a trial to one's temper, especially at night, as telephone lines are laid across it in most ingenious ways. First, there is a wire just at a suitable distance from the ground to trip you up into an especially filthy pool of wet mud. After getting up and walking carefully, picking your feet well up, a wire knocks your hat off, and manages to detach the badge, which entails a hunt of several minutes according to how far the badge had sunk in the mud and the distance that the hat has rolled. One proceeds again, and next runs hard up against a wire stretched tight across just at the height of your neck. After recovery you find one foot fastened in a mesh of wire in the clay. The worst of all are the cross-wires which are too high to step over and too low to step under easily with all one's field glasses, haversacks and maps, etc., hanging round one's neck. On finally reaching the O.P., completely worn out, you hurl yourself inside only to bump your head an awful whack on a low-lying cross-beam. So you lie prone, being slowly eaten by mosquitoes all over your face. These brutes are perfectly horrible. We have to report ourselves before leaving the Battery and telephone our arrival at the O.P., so that if more than three-quarters of an hour elapses before one has completed the one mile steeplechase, a search party can be sent out.

I ran into Morsehead of C Battery on one of these journeys last night when he suddenly had his walking stick knocked out of his hand by a shrapnel bullet.

The O.P. is merely part of a disused trench from which we have a fair view of the enemy lines. It is rather muddy with plenty of rats about. On several nights down at the Battery, when we had been fired at, we could distinctly see flashes of the enemy guns over the high ground to our right front [Hill 60]. We asked if we could engage this battery, but were told we must not because it was not in our zone, and naturally feel a bit sore about this.

Extracts From Diary

July 18 Got shelled at O.P., trench blown in 10 yards away.
   19 Got shelled at the Battery, five hits near B, C and D gun pits. Broke C's window which they had scrounged and were very proud of. Only one casualty; Gunner Capper got a blighty one. Had to go to Infantry trenches. Ran like a hare across an open road and caught foot in telephone wire. Reached Battalion H.Q. and hunted all over the place for the ends of our telephone wire. The Colonel a very nice fellow. Lost way coming back. Awful sweat. Heard there was to be an attack at 7 p.m. Attack began, din terrific, got fired on again. Over 300 shells in less

than half an hour—dugouts destroyed but guns all right, most fell 50 yards over. No one hurt. Dense smoke over Infantry trenches. Attack successful. Alert all night.

20 Went to O.P. Met Roger Poore of B Battery who had been down with the Infantry. Said the mine crater was 50 yards across. Many Germans blown to bits. Saw 17″ shell hit our trenches. Huge explosion. Returned to Battery. Infantry caught passing Suicide Corner. They asked us to bury a fellow whose back was blown in. Made us feel depressed. Gunner Lazzard lost his tea. Shrapnel knocked his mess tin he was drinking from out of his hand. Made us laugh!

21 Badly whizz-banged at dawn. Shelling increased during the day, mostly H.E. from 4 different batteries. The enemy can see our flashes but have not quite got our range. 90% of their shells drop just over us. Very little damage so far. Frazer and Butler wounded. German prisoners passed by us looking very dejected. Orders to move tonight. Raining hard.

CHAPTER 6

Menin Gate

Thanks awfully for the parcel from Fortnum and Mason. The dates will be just splendid when I go to the trenches as F.O.O., as the only things I can carry in my pockets are biscuits (dog variety). The Tommy's cooker has been a great boon, since without it I could have had only cold water which is dull fare for a week on end. It was all right subsisting on biscuits and water for our forty-eight hour spells, because of the luxury of the Battery to look forward to. The watch you sent me is simply grand. It keeps perfect time, and, what is more, I can check the time in the dark without having to strike the forbidden match.

We left our position by the lake soon after dark. It was hard work dragging out the guns and leading the teams up while falling into shell holes, etc. As usual, a wagon overturned, causing delay. We arrived at our new position about midnight in a storm of rain and worked like niggers to get the horses away before daylight. The water-cart horses took fright and ran down a bank into a moat. Luckily we managed to cut their traces before the water-cart sank and fished them out. D gun had to be dragged over some railway lines and down a bank. By 3 a.m. we were clear, soaked in mud and sweat. All next day we were hard at it trying to get straight. We tried to salvage the water-cart in the afternoon; I dived down to find the wheels buried in the mud and had some trouble fixing drag ropes to them. We tugged hard, but the drag ropes broke, so we had to leave it. Then I went straight up to the new O.P. and that evening actually saw some real live Germans through my telescope, about 2,000 yards off, so fired two rounds which scattered them. I was on duty all that night, with the signallers, to keep the telephone open for calls. On being relieved at 4 a.m., we had a drink of water and set off for the Infantry Headquarters (about half a mile from the trenches I wanted to get to). The Infantry Major there showed me his map of the trenches, which I compared with mine. Then I started off with the two signallers and a huge coil of wire, through the remains of a wood [Sanctuary Wood] to the trench I was aiming for, so as to open up communication with the Battery by 9.30. It was a fearful sweat as we had to do it in bits, pulling off 30 yards of wire, walk thirty yards carrying the coil weighing a hundredweight, and repeat the process for over a mile, by the devious way we had to go, in order to fix the wire safely. The poor signallers, Hobbs and Chandler, were quite exhausted but behaved like bricks. We had to press on, staggering over ditches, crawling through barbed wire and into trenches. We reached our goal exactly at 9.30, and got through to the Major. After observing his fire, I returned to Battalion Headquarters where I met Colonel Green who had commanded our O.T.C. Battalion when war broke out. Such a nice chap. He told me he had thought the officers at the O.T.C. camp (who, of course, were all schoolmasters) seemed rather a stodgy lot! He gave me a jolly nice lunch of ham and cake and told me to rest for a bit, but I had to go round the trenches and make a new map. I met fourteen officers of the Battalion, decent fellows, all of them. Roger Poore came to relieve me with two signallers that night, so we three staggered back, having had no sleep for three days. We found a G.S. wagon near our old position by the lake, which took us back to the Battery which we reached at midnight, and slept until 7.30 to find our Battery had been firing no less than six times during the night (one of the guns is only fifteen yards from my dugout, so, you see, I slept soundly!).

We continued to fire most of the day in answer to calls from the Infantry, in retaliation to those terrible *minen-werfers* [a large canister of H.E. which the Germans pitched over].

Several times we could not fire owing to orders not to fire if a German aeroplane happened to be around. They seem to be able to fly about just as they like.

Things are actually beginning to get a bit hot. We have nothing to compete with the Bosch in the way of trench mortars, and have to use any old thing we can lay hands on. To make things more unpleasant, they hold most of the high ground in a two to three mile semi-circle in front and to our flanks. In fact, we are in a sort of saucer.

The following came out in orders:

Trench howitzer introduced by 6th Corps named Toby. Used with great effect. Found in Paris and last used in 1700. Toby seemed highly pleased at being put on the active list after 200 years on the reserve list.

This afternoon I borrowed some tackle and pulleys from a heavy battery to salvage the water-cart. I dived in again and managed to hitch the hooks to the axles. After fixing the tackle to one of the poplars, we managed to haul it out safe and sound.

LIQUID FIRE ATTACK

At last I have a little time to try to tell you of the most strenuous and exciting week we spent in our last position. Some news of the battle has, I see, appeared in the papers.

Our position was overlooked by the enemy from Hill 60, about $2\frac{1}{2}$ miles to the south-east, and they certainly seemed to have unlimited ammunition to throw around.

In the evening after fishing out the water-cart, I went down to Sanctuary Wood again, taking some dates and biscuits to keep me going. On reaching Battalion Headquarters, I looked in on the two signallers to check our communications with the Battery. One of the officers invited me to share his dugout. It was curious listening, on that rainy night, to the intermittent rifle fire all round which sounded just like cricket practice at the school nets. At dawn, I went to the front trenches and got word from the Battery that it had been heavily shelled and that two of my men had been killed and C gun knocked out. Several other chaps had been wounded, including Roberts—hit in the spine. My job was to establish contact with the O.P. by signalling lamp. The trench was half enfiladed from a great stone wall at Hooge which was a nest of snipers. In order that the O.P., about a mile behind, could see where to look, I had taken along a white sheet about two feet square. I crept with this over the back of the trench and fixed it to the parados, a somewhat delicate operation. As the O.P. could not, of course, answer my signals because the Bosch would have spotted it, I did not know until the Battery started to register on the enemy trenches that all was well. Registering on various targets took nearly all day. The following morning I returned to the Battery covered in mud and filth to find C gun had been mended temporarily and was back on duty. The Major told me that it was a lucky thought about the white sheet, because, until he spotted it from the O.P., he had thought that the trench was our support trench instead of our front line, and that the German front line was our front line.

At the gun position, our dugouts were built into the embankment of the moat, on top of which ran the road, lined with poplars; our guns being on the other side. D gun was the furthest away—down a slope and over a railway embankment through which there was a small tunnel. We worked hard all that day and the next, strengthening the gun pits, carrying ammunition to the guns, deepening control posts and making a path by the water's edge to connect the dugouts, but were much hampered by German planes, when we had to stay motionless. We were greatly cheered when one of our newest and fastest planes swooped on a German one, setting it on fire. Ours looked as if it must have been travelling at over 100 miles an hour. We saw a German fall out and heard cheering from all over the place.

At dawn the following day, shortly before 4, we were woken by a most terrific shelling, with shells of every calibre. The whole place was rocking. The shelling seemed to increase in intensity and spurts of water were continually falling on my dugout. I felt fairly safe with my couch well against the bank. After some minutes a signaller suddenly appeared shoulting 'S.O.S.' I told him to call for five rounds battery fire, rushed to report to the Major, and then set off full tilt to the nearest gun and fired the first round to get things going. It is difficult to describe this extraordinarily intense time, which lasted about two hours, when we were firing as hard as our guns could go, while six German batteries of different calibres poured a hurricane of shells at us, determined to blot us out. Dazed by the concussion and noise, with the whole place thick with smoke, the men, stripped to the waist, had blackened and perspiring bodies. We had the thrill of nearly being killed ten times over without its depressing consequences, because the Bosch, who could, of course, see our flashes, must have thought our battery was on the moat side of the road and, with their accurate shooting, practically all the shells passed just over us. It seemed like being in a mighty football match. When the sudden lull came it felt as if one had just finished the hardest game of one's life. I went to my dugout for my boots (I had been rushing about in gym shoes) and found my sleeping bag ripped up by a hunk of shell-casing— a proof of the wisdom of early rising! We then had breakfast. Great joy among the men when they found they could fry bacon on the gun flanges! We had to chuck buckets of water down the barrels. It turned to steam at once. We then went all out to clear away the poplars strewn all over the road, to enable supplies of ammunition to reach us, and to repair damage to the gun pits and telephone wires.

At about 9 a.m., four teams bringing ammunition from the wagon lines galloped up. We unloaded the wagons at all speed to get the teams away. The 18-pounder shells were carried by the men across the broken ground to their guns, involving many journeys. At midday, another four teams arrived, and the same performance was repeated.

Evidently some of our trenches had been lost. We learned

from the wounded streaming by that the Germans had used liquid fire.

Orders came that a counter-attack was to be launched at three that afternoon, and I wondered if we could be so lucky again, because we were sure to have a repetition of that morning's storm. The only thing to do was to get what rest we could and make such preparations as possible.

The shelling had nearly stopped and, after seeing the ammunition into the gun pits and the hundreds of empty shell cases chucked into ditches, I went to report to the Major and found him under a pile of earth except for his head. The roof of his dugout had been blown in. I thought he was dead, but, instead, he was fast asleep! He had turned in for a nap before the next bout and dimly remembered feeling a sudden weight on his body and thinking, 'Oh! How dreadful!' he went fast asleep again! It was so ludicrous that we both laughed.

That afternoon, the battle was even hotter. The enemy had turned a heavy high velocity battery on to us for good measure. As it was impossible to be heard more than two or three yards off in that pandemonium, and as the telephone lines to the guns were cut, my job was to take orders from the telephone dugout where the Major was and rush from gun to gun to shout them to each. How I ran! Down came more poplars all stripped of their branches by then. Several times the men of A gun had to rush out and pull away trees from the road to allow ammunition teams to gallop by. One shell caught the back of a wagon of 6-inch shells. It exploded, blowing out the back of the wagon which helped the team to gallop faster. I was just emerging from A gun to cross the road, when I was blown backwards off my feet, landing on my back across the gun trail, but quite unhurt much to the surprise of the men. They told me later that some silly remark I made then put them into good heart again. Their gun was nearest the road and they were just about at the end of their tether, expecting any second to be blown to bits.

In the middle of all this row, eight wagon loads galloped up to within fifty yards. Two men from each gun, with the help

47

of the cooks and spare signallers and, of course, the drivers, feverishly pulled out the shells and threw them into the ditch by the roadside so as to get the teams away. Then there was the job of running with the shells to the gun pits where stocks were getting short. D gun was most difficult to reach. We ran with a shell under each arm, dropping flat on our faces when shells fell very close. While nearing D gun on one of these trips, a shell came with the usual roar. I thought it would fall, like most of the others, some thirty yards over, so took no notice, but at the last second I realized my mistake and fell flat just in time, to be buried with earth and winded for a few seconds. I then started working my shoulders to free myself, and finally stood up to see one of the gunners who was some twenty yards away looking as if he had seen a ghost. He had seen the explosion and when the smoke lifted I had disappeared and then reappeared like a phoenix from under the earth forming the lip of the crater. Begrimed, sweating and deaf, so we continued our labours.

The gunners were having a hard time to keep their guns working, and had to push them back after each round because the oil in the hydraulic mechanism was too hot. The empty shell cases had to be thrown out of the pits anywhere to give elbow room. The fitter, a mere boy, did wonderful work. Often I saw him as he emerged from the smoke running from gun to gun as they kept breaking down. Men with buckets were rushing to their guns to sluice them down. The roof of A gun caved in from the volume of water thrown up from the moat, and D gun had its roof blown off.

Finally, at about five, the lull came. We found all our dugouts had been blown in, but what a miraculous escape we had had due to the accuracy of the enemy guns dropping nearly all their shells on the road and the moat behind. Only four of our men were killed that afternoon, but what a four they were, all trained gun-layers whom we could ill afford to lose. These, with their gallant fellow Gunner Albert, who had taken an urgent message on the Battery cycle to Brigade Headquarters by the Menin Gate during the morning hate and had his head removed by a shell on his way back, we buried that evening behind the guns. The Major read the service. Together with the seven wounded, we lost about a third of our men that day. It could have been much worse.

During the lull, our guns continued slow battery fire at two minute intervals. I went over to see the effect of a direct hit on some railway lines three or four yards in front of D gun. Suddenly the gun fired, knocking me flat on my face (the crew, of course, did not see me because the guns were laid on aiming posts to the rear). The shell must have passed a foot or so over my head. My hair was singed and I was deaf as a post for the rest of that evening.

We received word later that a further supply of ammunition had arrived at Brigade Headquarters about 500 yards off. We took the hand cart at the double, as the road was still being shelled, to collect what we could. The Colonel looked very worn out. By the end of that day, the Brigade had fired an average of 1,000 rounds per gun—equivalent to twelve times their own weight—all brought up from the Brigade Ammunition Column some 10 miles away—a wonderful feat. At 9 p.m. four more wagons of ammunition arrived. We broke for a rest at 10 p.m., but had to stand to at 10.30 with orders to fire all night, increasing the rate during the hours before dawn. Things were quieter when we stood down at 6 a.m. I had time to gobble some breakfast before starting off to the O.P. to relieve Lennox, who had just returned from the trenches. He gave me a grim picture of the position there. The counter-attack had not gone well, only a few trenches being retaken. Most of our two rifle battalions we had been covering had been killed, wounded or burnt. Cousin Harry was missing. Huge casualty lists of these two regiments have since appeared in the papers. The men had tried to face the first liquid fire attack by manning the trenches, but the next time they knew better and lay low, letting the fire pass over them. As soon as it stopped they leapt up in time to repel the Huns following behind.

I remembered those two Battalions and how cheerily they sang as they marched to the station at Aldershot only two months before. Lennox said our shooting had been splendid, mowing down scores of the enemy.

From there, I pushed on to the trenches meeting batch after batch of wounded wandering slowly back, some trying to help others. They all looked done in, quite unconscious of the shelling, often falling when hit for the second time. Among them was Captain de Mowbray. He could hardly speak. The effect of seeing all these poor chaps looking so utterly crushed made the tears start streaming down my cheeks. A man with his leg blown off seemed in great pain, but when I was going to give him a morphia stamp from that little book of medicinal stamps you sent me, an orderly told me he had already had a shot and thought it unwise to give him more. It is quite maddening that in the face of all this devilry ever invented, of bombs, mortars, gas, liquid fire and machine guns galore, all our fellows have is the old rifle. If we could but meet the Germans on equal terms how we should whack them!

On reaching the wood all was chaos. Dead and dying everywhere with stretcher bearers knocked out. I went off with the two signallers in search of our wire. We had to crawl, as we were in view of the enemy from both flanks. Each of us went in a different direction and we eventually found it. When we tapped in there was no answer so I sent Peel to mend the wire up towards the O.P. while Coltman and I followed it down towards Zouave Wood where the Germans were.

We tapped off at dusk and laid fresh wire across a field as far as it would go, returning afterwards to Battalion H.Q. We were woken by a heavy bombardment and were given rifles as an attack was expected. Nothing happened, however, and at dawn we luckily found the end of the wire we had left the day before and to our delight managed to get through to the O.P. The whole of that day we were kept at it repairing our lines as they were cut, and directing the fire of the Battery. We managed to borrow two reels of black wire from the Infantry which took us right to Battalion H.Q. where I had orders to remain. It was then nearly midnight. I had just managed to get some supper for my signallers when a sergeant reported that they had captured a 'parson dressed up as an officer' coming from the enemy lines. The Colonel said, 'Show him in'. He was a very tall man with a gaunt face who said his name was Talbot [he started Toc H] and that he had been crawling in from no-man's-land where he had found the body of his brother. He showed us his brother's cigarette case with a hole through it which he had taken from the breast pocket. He looked done in, so I gave him the tea I had got for the signallers. Shortly afterwards a message came through that some of our shells had hit our infantry. I got through to Cavanagh, our Adjutant, saying that I thought the shells were Hun shells from Hill 60 to our right. He confirmed that none of our Brigade had fired in that sector. I sent Peel off to Cavanagh with the latest map I had made, showing our and the German trenches, because all was in rather chaos.

Just before dawn, I met Elton of D Battery who said he was to hand over to me and left me with his signaller which pleased me. Although I worked the life out of him, we were still too short-handed to retrieve our things. After a busy day and night of it, Lennox turned up to relieve me, and I and my signallers staggered back to Battery. We were so dead beat that we went each at our own pace and took no heed of shelling. On reaching the Battery late that afternoon, Thomas, our new subaltern, a very nice fellow, greeted me, saying the Major was going to fire, but suggested I get some rest. I scraped the top layer of mud off. My socks stuck to my feet. After a bathe in the moat and some food, I dropped off to sleep at 6.30, to be wakened with vigorous shaking two hours later to report to the Major. My eyes were so puffed I could hardly see out of them.

The Major told me that we were to be relieved that night and that I was to move my section first. When the relief Battery arrived, our limbers had not turned up, so we had to borrow theirs. It was after midnight when we reached our new position, where we hurriedly unlimbered, shoved the guns into a hedge and just dropped to sleep as we were, for a solid six hours! Our first real sleep for five days.

This is a quiet sector, and we have been able to get our guns dug in and registered without disturbance. News has come of the promotion of Sergeant-Major Alexander of the Brigade Ammunition Column, to the rank of Acting Captain for the way he organized that remarkable supply of ammunition during the recent excitement. Apparently, the Captain was away in Poperinghe when the S.O.S. came through and is to be court martialled. The story goes that, when he did turn up, Alexander said to him: 'You can clear off—I am in command here,' or words to that effect.

1. The author photographed at Arras, 1916.

2. 'Uncle Julian' – Brigadier-General J. D. Tyndale-Biscoe.

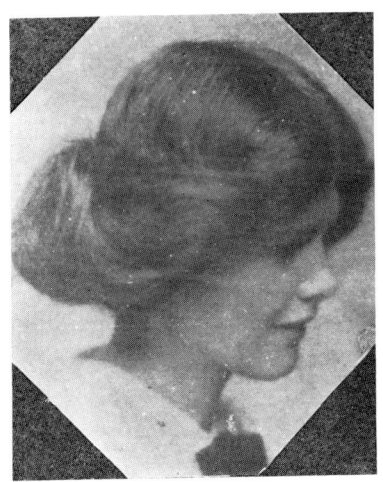

3. Cousin Julie Langdale-Smith.

4. The author's brother, Harold, with his aircraft.

5. *The uncles, fifteen years later. From left to right: Albert, RA;
Teddie, RN; Julian, 11th Hussars; Arthur, 9th Hampshires.*

6. *Capt. Soames, commanding
A Battery, 48th Brigade, 14th
Division, killed in action on the
Somme, September, 1916.*

7. *A. C. Cooper at a fête in Dublin.
He lost an arm in France but
managed to return for the Somme
offensive, where he lost part of a
foot. He returned to France yet
again, and died as a result of being
gassed.*

CHAPTER 7

From Pillar to Post

GARDEN POINT

We are having a fairly uneventful time here. I am at present doing the O.P. stretch. We have a bath and change every three days at the Battery. Our new O.P. is a small dugout about three feet high with just room for the maps and field-glasses on one side, telescope in the centre, and the foodstuffs and tommy's cooker on the other. We have potted meat, Maconachi, biscuits, cake, butter, tea and Oxo, so don't do badly.

While at our first O.P. last week, and all seemed quite peaceful, the Huns, for some reason, decided to strafe us—five or six salvoes—that was all. I had just gone along the trench to C Battery's dugout to report to the Colonel who was with Captain Walker and a subaltern when a shell came right in. Fortunately it was a dud and we only suffered some bruises. On return, I found our O.P. was totally wrecked. On being relieved by Thomas later, I went to the Battery for a wash before going down to the trenches which are very comfortable. After doing some registering for the Major, we heard great cheering from the Germans all along their lines. Suddenly they stuck up placards, saying: Warsaw Has Fallen. The Infantry amused themselves taking pot shots at them.

Yesterday I was with the Infantry. The Colonel was most friendly and insisted that I should mess with him and the Adjutant.

At the Battery, we live in the lap of luxury. I get there about 9.30 and have a leisurely breakfast, bath in an old tub and change. Then inspection of the guns and some firing to while away the time between meals. At about 10 p.m., the ammunition arrives with the cook's cart bringing letters.

Some Georges (11 inch and 13 inch) and a Jack Johnson (17 inch) passed over the other day. The Jack Johnson roared over like a train going at 80 m.p.h. into Ypres, half a mile off, but must have caught sight of us on the way because its base came hurtling back all the way, landing near our mess. We dug it up. It is an enormous piece of iron, weighing about the same as I do!

Thanks awfully for the boxing gloves. They will come in handy when we have another spell out of the line. Meanwhile, we have a piano and gramophone to amuse us. We are well hidden in a garden. My dugout is under a flower bed with some small fruit trees on the top.

The only snag here is that we have been bothered with lice in this new position. These little brutes are not too obtrusive, but difficult to get rid of as they are almost too small to see. It is unpleasant to feel that they are moving about inside our clothes. The men, when off duty, take their shirts off and have a good hunt. On Monday I spent most of the day in the saddle going first to Abbeville for money and then to the wagon lines to pay the men there. While there, I took the opportunity, as an anti-lice measure, to get my groom to cut off all my hair with the horse-clippers. On the way back to the gun position, I looked in at Brigade Headquarters where I was greeted with loud guffaws. I must say my head feels odd—bristly and rather itchy.

Such a nice fellow has been transferred to us from B Battery. He is Roger Poore, son of the Admiral. He served in the Navy for five years and then went rubber planting in Ceylon until war broke out when he joined up. He has been with the Brigade for over a year, but I never got to know him well before now. He is ten years older than I with the energy and enterprise that Navy men always have. He and I are busy making a wash-house and drying-room for the men. We have procured some wooden tubs from the town and are rigging up a hot water system with the aid of pipes and an old tank.

Leave has started. I may get mine in three or four months.

We get three days clear in England, I think. At the present rate of leave for the men (1 per cent at a time), the last lot will be getting theirs about two years hence. Terrible thought—they may never get it because the war may be over before their turn comes!

General Sandys has just come as our C.R.A. in place of General Princep. He seems a most friendly sort of man. The Colonel introduced me to him and he made me feel quite at ease. He said he knew you and Uncle Albert.

We were having a bit of shelling one morning when a shell burst in the entrance of the Major's dugout. I rushed in to find him on his back with his legs in the air. He had been blown over backwards while sitting on his chair. He picked himself up quite unhurt thinking it a great joke. Luckily, he happened to be just round the corner from the entrance. His bed and the rest of his stuff were knocked to pieces. Our garden seat went west and I rushed to see if our Harrods box was intact. Thank goodness, it was.

Many of us here were very sorry to see the name of Brigadier-General Street among those killed recently in Gallipoli. He was our O.C. for a short while at Godalming and we all thought him a wonderful fellow.

GLASS HOUSES

The Battery went out for a short spell at the end of last month. When we arrived at our billets, we found some German rifle ammunition. There was the usual stove in the middle of the living room. I left one of these bullets standing on its base on top of the stove and forgot about it. That evening the stove was lighted and the Major, Parry, Lennox and I sat down by it for a game of vingt-et-un. Suddenly, there was a startling report causing the other three to jump out of their seats. It came to me in a flash what I had done so did not jump so high. I suppose the bullet must have gone through the roof. At any rate, we all discussed what could have caused the bang and were completely mystified, because I naturally did not divulge the secret!

Parry told us a delightful story about Captain (ex Sergeant-Major) Alexander, O.C., the Brigade Ammunition Column. The Column had just dismounted in a village street in front of Brigade Headquarters where the Colonel and several others were, when they heard a muffled expletive from one of the drivers—a horse had probably trodden on his foot—followed by a mighty roar from Alexander, which could be heard right down the street. 'Stop that swearing, *Damn you!* Can't you speak like a *gentleman,* you foul-mouthed *B . . . . R!!*'

We have now come into action in a mining district and there is an old shaft behind A gun about eight feet wide and of unknown depth, across which we placed two planks to connect it with the control post some ten yards behind.

Late one evening last week, we suddenly had orders to fire. Something delayed A gun which should have fired first, thus delaying the whole proceeding. I rushed out of my post shouting blue murder, missed my footing on the planks and over I went. Luckily my foot was caught by the ankle and there I was, hanging head downwards. From my inverted position I heard the Major, who by then had reached the gun in a rage, asking where I was, and Sergeant Grant's reply of, 'I don't know, sir, but we *heard* him just now.' They looked around, and seeing my foot, fished me out. No bones broken, and apart from a limp for a day or two, I was all right.

SIDE SHOW FOR LOOS

Things are hotting up here. We shall be doing such things that the ears of all them that hear shall tingle.

Three days ago I was called at the O.P. at 1 a.m. to expect an attack, and watched with all eyes till dawn. Then I heard a complete roar of shells passing over and bursting in the region of where I fancied our Battery was, so phoned them up to report that shells appeared to be falling on them, and got a rude reply that they were! After going to the Infantry, I returned to the

Battery to find the whole place churned up, but no casualties. C Battery on our left got it worst. Both their subalterns had been hit. One had both legs blown off. I saw him for a moment: he was not in pain—too numbed, I suppose—but he knew he was finished. He was quite cheerful and smoking a cigarette, but died soon afterwards.

We shifted our position that night and worked till four next morning when I went to the O.P. We fired, off and on, all that day and night. On the first day of our strafe, the Brigade sent down three F.O.O.s to the trenches. Only one returned. Dear old Roger Poore was one of the casualties. The signallers brought his body here and we buried him in a ground sheet. Anyhow, there is one thing to be thankful for—he had just been on leave to see his fiancée and so spent his last week happily, but bad luck on her.

Yesterday, four of us went down, and two of us returned. (It must be a job to keep replacing subalterns at this rate.) When I reported to the Infantry Colonel, a nasty fellow, he said: 'I suppose you have come to take the place of Hayter, who has just been killed.' I told him that I had not heard about Hayter, and moved off without further civilities. Our Battery is concentrating on twenty-five yards of trench, and I saw engaging that same sector, 4·5 inch hows, 6 inch hows and 9·2 inch hows. Not bad! There is not one sandbag on another. All our trenches are knocked in. I had to crawl over them and had my first experience of a *minen-werfer*. I did not see it, but heard it coming—a sort of woof-woof noise, as it turned head over heels in the air. I was lying flat when it landed, but the concussion lifted me up and threw me down, and I was quite winded for a few moments. On reaching the front trench, I met the F.O.O. of the 9·2 inch battery. It was quite quiet there, like the eye of a cyclone, with all hell fore and aft of us. It quite fascinated me to watch the accuracy of his shells obliterating what was left of the German trenches, blowing up about five yards at a time. I saw three Germans blown into the air together.

All our telephone lines had, of course, been blown to bits.

I then saw, to my surprise, my signaller, Gunner Miles, appearing out of the smoke behind us. He came to give me a verbal message from the Major, to return at once. How he reached me in one piece, I can't think; a most imperturbable fellow, who won a Military Medal during some excitement we had nearly two months ago. We waited until things were quieter before returning.

Today I was on the run over an unhealthy bit of ground, and it was all I could do to avoid treading on the limbs of poor devils who had been blown to bits. Our zone is looked upon with horror by the troops out here, but still it must be worse in the Dardanelles.

COMMINES CANAL

We came out of action last month after a pretty hefty battle. Our Division launched an attack on the 25th, after giving the enemy every reason to suppose we would. This was to draw off their troops from the major attack at Loos. In spite of this, we captured several lines of trenches. Our guns fired like billy-o and got hot enough to fry bacon. After an overhaul of our guns, etc., we returned to a new sector.

Those Gilgit boots you sent me are simply splendid, they could not be better. Never will I be troubled with cold feet this winter—at least, I hope not!

It has been very quiet here. The Major and I went down to reconnoitre the German trenches. We noticed an old ruin about 300 yards behind our front line which looked a likely place from which to get a good view, so we got out of the trench and stalked towards it, but the Bosch soon spotted us and let fly, so we hurried back on all fours. The Major looked so funny, running like that with his smart gaiters on and a cigar in his mouth!

Two Alsatians deserted from the Germans and gave themselves up the other day. They were awfully bucked and said 'Bonjour' to everyone.

Our new subaltern in place of Roger Poore is a man named

Chadwick. He is a ranker and seems to be a good sort.

We were very short of sandbags about six weeks ago. I had heard from the sewing party in Godalming, saying they would like to send out some comforts for our battery and asked what we would like. I told them we were well off for socks and mufflers, etc., but we were short of sandbags, and it would help towards the safety of our men if we could get some. I heard later from [cousin] Dorothy that they had dispatched 8,000! We never got them. Now we have had a bit of a snorter from the D.A.Q.M.G. about this package, saying that the shortage of sandbags was due to transport difficulties only. Anyway, we seem to have as many as we want now.

I have just heard that I have got my second pip.

Major Erskine left us last month. We were naturally very sad. He has been given command of a Horse Battery with the Third Cavalry Division. Captain Soames is our new O.C. He is about thirty, and has just come from a Horse Battery. Captain Walker of C Battery has been given the Legion of Honour, which has pleased us all.

I have just been playing over a rather cracked record which dear old Roger Poore liked so much. It has a delightful tune, but rather sad in its way. It brings him to mind so vividly. He was almost like an elder brother to me. I shall treasure that record.

Yesterday I climbed about sixty feet up a factory chimney that is still standing, in order to spot for some red signals that were being tried out. It was a weird feeling up there, as the chimney rocked when shells fell near, and it was quite a relief to get back to *terra firma* again.

Things are pretty quiet at present, and we have made ourselves very comfortable with bits of furniture we have picked up among the ruins.

I have invented a home-made flashspotter for the O.P., with a ruler notched to represent every 100 yards as per our map. The ruler is pivoted to the point on the map where our O.P. is. We just point the ruler at gun flashes at night, take the time on a stopwatch till the sound comes, run a pencil along the ruler the number of notches indicated, and there, approximately, is the enemy battery.

Captain Soames went on leave on the 14 November. On the day he left, we had orders to prepare a new position and cover the new zone as soon as possible. As our Battery had to continue in action where they were, I left Lennox in charge and took a sergeant, a signaller and sixteen men from the wagon lines, leaving them one man to three horses. With these men, we worked night and day. It rained nearly the whole time and we had to fill the sandbags with wet clay. Wagons full of materials for the gun pits arrived each night. These we unloaded and filled the returning wagons with bricks from a ruin, for our horse lines which were turning into a quagmire, and were twelve miles to our rear. Just as a wagon was leaving one night, the road gave way by the side of a ditch, and into it went the wagon with the horses. The ditch was so deep and narrow that it took two and a half hours of our precious time to dig them out.

In between whiles, I had to find a new O.P., to visit the Infantry we were to cover and, with the signaller, to lay the wires. Two men had to leave work at the gun position to bury the wires. The men had to work all night and, after a two-hour rest, all day, with a break of one hour for food, sometimes at 1 p.m. and once at 4 p.m. They were, of course, wet to the skin the whole time as the rain hardly ever let up. At times I thought they would break down, but they stuck to it like Trojans. After five days we brought the guns across and into the pits which we had been most careful to cover each day with foliage. Communications with the O.P. and Infantry were perfect, but when all was ready to register, down came the fog which lasted two days. It was maddening, but, on the morning the Captain returned, it cleared and at last I was able to see the German trenches, and fired thirty-six rounds taking some big chinks out of their parapets.

The Captain expressed great surprise that so much had been done.

Last week, when I went up to the O.P., the rats made a beeline for the grub in my pockets. In spite of my knocking them away, they managed to eat it all up when I dozed off—so I had 'nowt' for breakfast.

Our mess is in the remains of a farmhouse, part of which still has a roof. We are at present most comfortable sitting round a roaring log fire. Just like Christmas!

A funny thing happened last night. When sitting with Chadwick in our mess, I suddenly felt a queer attack of cold feet coming on for no reason at all. I told Chadwick how I felt, and said that if the Bosch should pitch some shells over, I would run like a hare. Almost immediately a salvo came over, and one shell hit the side of our house. Off I went like a long-dog, with Chadwick, who had obviously been infected by my nerves, close behind. Out we ran into the rain, laughing quite uncontrollably and falling into shell holes until we sort of sobered up, and walked back quietly, wondering rather shamefacedly whatever had come over us. It was luck that it was a filthy dark night.

CHAPTER 8

Mostly Mud

About ten days ago the Captain told me to go to the wagon lines, as the Sergeant-Major had reported trouble among the drivers. The continual rain had turned the whole field into a quagmire. The mud was almost knee deep. It was only by walking with care, lifting one leg up slowly at a time, that it was possible to avoid wet mud overlapping the tops of one's gumboots. The drivers had nothing but oatsacks as cover, which, of course, was no use against the rain. Into these makeshift quarters they had to take their harness in order to try to clean it, often late into the night by the light of candles. Of course, it was always covered in mud as soon as it was used again. Apparently one of the drivers had suddenly shouted: 'I'm b . . . . . . d if I clean any more bleeding 'arness', and threw his cap at the candles, knocking them out, whereupon all the others downed harness.

When the Sergeant-Major brought the culprit to me, I remembered old Princep reading to us about all the crimes that could be committed, so picked up an official tome and pretended to read from it: 'While on active service inciting to mutiny, maximum punishment death', and then told him this was much too serious for me to deal with and ordered him to be taken, with the ammunition wagons, under escort to the O.C. that night. I gave the escort a letter to the Captain, explaining the appalling conditions under which the drivers were living, and suggested that a bit of a wigging was all that was wanted.

I have been dashing about, trying to get materials to give some protection from the rain to the men in their catsack bivouacs. Three nights ago I caught a road railway train about midnight, going to a town. When it slowed down a bit, I clutched at an old truck and scrambled in. It took me past where I wanted to go and was going too fast for me to jump out. I was carried about ten miles before I could get off, and was starting to walk back in the pouring rain when, suddenly, a man came trotting by on a mule, leading a spare one. I jumped on, and rode it bareback trotting hard all the way, getting in at dawn, when I bumped into O'Keefe whom I had met at the Shop. He kindly gave me a bath and some breakfast. I managed to procure two large bundles of fifty groundsheets each, which will be a help.

The only entry in my diary for the last seven days or so has been confined to just one word—'M U D'.

The Battery came out last week. The mud is much the same. Anyhow, we get plenty of exercise, walking about the camp, especially after a dry day when the mud thickens. We sink up to about one inch below the knee and then put the other foot in and pull hard till we get the first one out, taking great care that the gumboot is not pulled right off. The Captain keeps himself remarkably spruce in all this, and uses a walking stick.

I am sleeping in a tent now, and have put mud all round the sides which keeps it quite warm. My valise is on an old door which is placed on top of two boxes to keep it above the mud. One night it tipped up, but luckily my valise is pretty mudproof.

We had to stand to last week as the Germans made a gas attack, but it failed.

We celebrated Christmas with a big blow-out for the men in a large marquee we had borrowed. Just before dinner, the Captain and we three subs went along to wish them a happy Christmas. Just as the Captain had finished his little speech, some wag enlivened proceedings by shouting the command: 'F-E-E-E-D!'

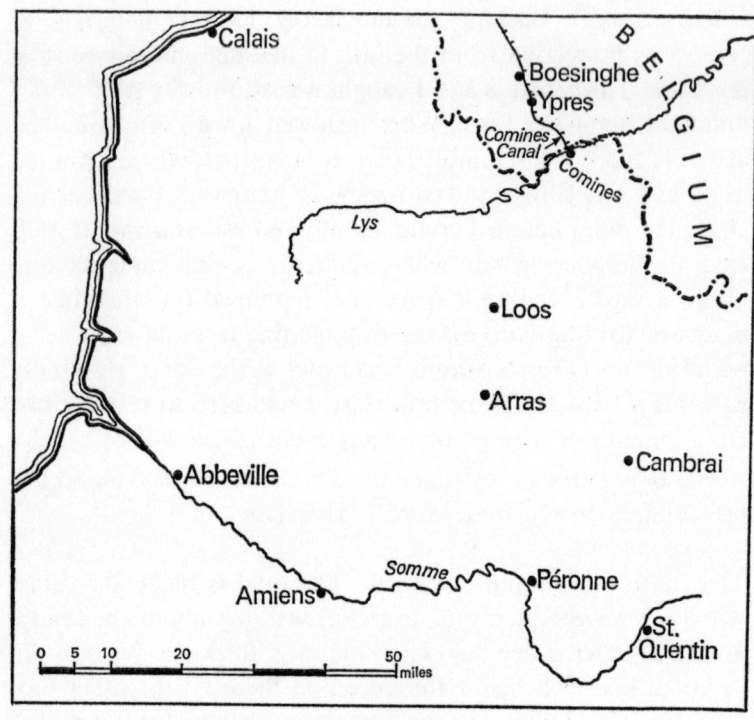

Ypres and the Somme, 1916

BOESINGHE

We came into action again after Christmas, in a bleak and dismal part of the line, too flat to find a suitable O.P. The mud is awful, water level being ground level. Such trenches as have not disintegrated are filled with mud and water. At the O.P., which is in the remains of a trench, one stands up to one's waist in mud and water. During the nights we are there, the signaller and I keep lifting each foot in turn out of the water to massage it to prevent getting trench feet. Yesterday morning there was a thin layer of ice on the water in the trench.

The Captain came in the morning, and brought us some rum which was most reviving. He told me he wanted me to go that night to trace the whereabouts of our front line. I went off with one signaller. It was a bit of a nightmare trying to find our way. We staggered across the muddy waste, falling into shell holes full of water. We came across the body of a Tommy lying in one—he had evidently fallen in and could not get out. Our gumboots were soon sucked off, and several times we had to help each other up. We kept on aided, on occasions, by Very lights and rifle flashes. We could not pick out trenches, as they were merely ditches. Then we saw several flashes together, and thought that must be our front line. We were making for it, and had just stepped across a ditch, when I heard low voices, so we stopped to ask where the front line was. One of them whispered to us to keep quiet, saying they were a listening post in front of our front line. It was lucky we heard them, as we were making straight for the German front line and that would have been the end of us, at any rate until the end of the war. On the way back, we lost our way and had to swim across a battered and slimy canal [the Ysar]—not easy in greatcoats and gear. We got in just after dawn this morning. After a wash, I reported to the Captain, who told me I am to go on leave the day after tomorrow.

I can hardly believe it and told him: 'No more crossing trenches for me. I will rather swim along their bottoms until I am safely off!'

I have just returned from leave. It has all been like a dream. Straight from this mud, living more like drowned rats, if that is possible, to the lights of Piccadilly and a gorgeous play at a theatre, and with more money than I could spend. What a rush it all was—no time to waste in sleeping. I have come back to the front for a rest!

I left Poperinghe on the morning train on the 7th, and arrived at Bologne at mid-day—caught the staff boat at 3.30 and was in Waterloo that night where I had a Turkish Bath. Then went off to see [cousin] Mollie at Oxford where she is at school, and had lunch with the Bartons. Mollie and I cycled off to see the Langdale-Smith cousins at Holton, and had tea there, getting back for supper. I caught the train to London and put up at the Grosvenor. Next morning I went to church with the Mitchells, when I nearly tipped the man, who turned out to be our host that night, for giving me a prayer book on the way in. Called on Great Aunt Mary in the afternoon. She insisted on giving me £2. Then I went to Sister Agnes's Hospital in Belgrave Square to see Cousin Harry. He seemed in excellent spirits and hopes to be able to do some mountain-climbing again after the war, in spite of losing half his leg. I also called on Uncle L'Estrange, where I met Sam Bakaal, who is with the Y.M.C.A. Next morning was spent in shopping and gulping in the sights of old London. I called on Mrs Hadow, who advised me about theatre shows, and then went to the Piccadilly, where I heard Norman was, and luckily found him in the bar. He had his back to me, so I laid my stick across his shoulders, and he was quite surprised. He was with a friend, and after much talking at an enormous rate, we decided to go to a play that night. After lunch I rang up [cousin] Nata to come too, and booked a box at the Gaiety. We all had a scrumptious dinner and then squashed into our box where we saw 'Tonight's the Night', with Leslie Henson and George Grossmith. It was gorgeous—grand cheery songs and much laughter. What a wonderful ending to my leave! Dear Uncle Albert came to the station to see me off next morning. Dobbie was also on his way back, so we travelled together. The boat journey back was rough. I rushed down to the sick room where I saw a general and two staff officers all being sick. This so surprised and tickled me that I suddenly felt quite all right again.

I reached Poperinghe that night, and got a comfortable shake-down at Talbot House and had a friendly welcome from the Padre.

Next morning, I reached our wagon lines, and found one of my drivers tied to a wagon wheel. I gave him a friendly greeting, saying, 'Hello you old rascal—what have you been up to now?'

He replied with a wry grin. He was subject to drinking bouts and had probably overstepped the mark. He was not uncomfortable, as the straps to his wrists and feet were quite loose.

I learned that the Battery had moved to a new position, and got here last night. It is a fairly comfortable spot, with a bit of a farmhouse for living quarters. There is no digging down for dugouts these days, because we are only six inches above water level. We have managed to get a lot of iron girders to roof our gun pits, on which we put about four layers of sandbags and then some building rubble.

Did I tell you about pamphlets called *'Die Feld Post'* dropped from an aeroplane? I saw them floating down on the way to the trenches and picked them up—all about riots in Berlin.

Last week a word came for me to report to the C.R.A. Corps Headquarters in three hours' time, so I rushed down on a push bike and was taken to General Paget. He said, 'Do you want a regular commission?' He told me that General Sandys had recommended me for appointment as First Lieutenant (instead of Second Lieutenant as is normal), and that he proposed to forward this recommendation. Is not General Sandys an old brick?

I had tea there, and happened to mention the German pamphlets. They were very interested and forwarded them to Army Headquarters with all details. The Intelligence Major asked me how I had come, and kindly arranged for a motor to take me back. He showed me a lot of interesting trophies, so I thoroughly enjoyed myself. They live in a beautiful chateau. The old Count and his family live there, too.

Three days later I was told to report to G.H.Q. at St Omer. On the train I met a very nice fellow called Southey, who said that he had also been told to report about a regular commission. On arrival, we were ushered into a waiting-room to see General Headlam. Southey went in first. I then went in, and felt a bit nervous at being in the presence of such a big pot. He was very pleasant, and asked me a number of questions, but I still felt that the mere word 'sir' was not enough for such as he and to make up for it kept saying 'sir' on every possible occasion. He must have thought me rather childish. Anyhow, we shall see what we shall see. Southey and I travelled back together as far as Poperinghe where we had a pleasant supper together last night.

ELVERDINGHE

The Bosch sent over some gas shells the other day, which made us all weep. One hit the sergeants' mess, but did little damage. The next day we were provided with the usual spectacle of a Zeppelin passing over us on its way back to Germany. It off loaded a few bombs which made a great noise.

I went up to the O.P. with a signaller during the night to cut down a large tree which was obstructing our view about a quarter of a mile ahead, and managed to fell it just before dawn. On returning to the O.P., I found the Captain. We stayed there all day and fired several hundred rounds. We returned to the Battery at 10 p.m., but were called out before 4 a.m. and fired several hundreds more rounds as the enemy were trying to be nasty. The Captain left again before dawn for the O.P.; I was left in charge of the guns, and we did a lot of firing in the early morning. Then we were shelled. The Huns started pitching them near No. 4 gun, so I moved the men to No. 3. The next salvo pitched near No. 3, so I moved them to Nos. 1 and 2. It was awfully funny to see the orderly running behind the men with the breakfast—a great dixie of tea and a pile of bacon. The next salvo put No. 3 gun out of action. As we had to increase rate of firing, I sent No. 4 gun crew back again. It was hard work with wagons of ammunition galloping up at all hours. Several French ammunition wagons galloped past us—a great sight. We ran out of oil for buffers once, which incapacitated another gun for a few minutes, and the place caught fire, but we soon put it out. Three of our men were killed. Bombardier Tracey of my section, and one of the finest men we had, had the top of his skull whipped off. I saw him lying there breathing as if in a

68

8. *Hauling guns in the mud (Imperial War Museum).*

9. *Snow march to Arras, when seven and a half miles were covered in thirteen hours (Imperial War Museum).*

10. *A common type of OP, the Somme, 1916 (Imperial War Museum).*

11. *The shattered Cloth Hall at Ypres, subsequently restored after the war (Imperial War Museum).*

peaceful sleep. Just after we buried them that evening, a salvo hit the place, so we had to bury them again. I felt very bad about Tracey: he was a devout chap. When censoring one of his letters I could not help being tickled by the way he had ended it with the words, 'May God preserve you from your loving husband'. I am writing to his widow to say how much we all admired and liked him, but I fear it will be poor consolation to her.

We have left Tom's Dog behind us for good and all. The Battery had been agog with rumours for some time that we might be leaving, ever since all our horses were malleined two months ago. Everyone is fearfully pleased about it, singing and shouting all day long. We marched the whole day and are now living in the lap of luxury. The horses are in a grass field. I have the best room in the best house in the village—a feather bed and embroidered sheets, a carpet, chairs and a silver looking-glass. This morning we went for a rough exercise (i.e. no saddles, just blankets). I gave them a good long trot that warmed us all up.

I am going to turn in to sleep in that lovely bed. As a matter of fact, I sleep just as soundly anywhere. The night before last on the stone floor in a draughty ruin with no blankets, just my clothes and overcoat, I slept the sleep of the just!

PART THREE

Arras, The Somme and Blighty
March to December 1916

CHAPTER 9

Arras

It had been one of the busiest and most interesting fortnights I have ever spent. We had sudden orders to entrain at 1.30 a.m. at a certain station and set off at 8.30 p.m. On the way, one of our guns got ditched with the horses struggling in the mud. It was taking so long to get them out that the Captain decided that he must go on with the rest of the Battery, and told me to bring on the casualty as soon as possible. He left me with six gunners. With these and the three drivers, we managed to right the gun and horses after a bit of a struggle, and set off at a fast trot. I was not too sure of the way, but followed what seemed to be the most recent tracks and reached the station just before the train, to the great relief of the Captain. It was quite a job hauling the guns and horses on board from ground level, especially as many of the horses were frightened.

We reached our destination after about nine hours, unloaded the guns and horses from the train [near Amiens] and, after a march of fourteen miles, got in at 7 p.m., the men having had nothing to eat for nearly twenty-four hours. The horses were watered and remained in a field. The men occupied two barns. We were given quite a comfortable room. We expected to stay here some time and started training in open warfare. Two days later, at breakfast, we got orders to move at any minute and by 11 were on the road—quite hilly country. When we reached our destination that night, we found the town full of troops and had much difficulty in finding barns for the men. It was freezing and snowing hard.

We were up at five next morning, when it was still snowing and freezing. We harnessed up at 11. The harness was covered with snow. The ice on the pond was thick enough to walk on and took some breaking for the horses to drink. By the time we started, the snow lay three or four inches deep. It got beaten down by the traffic and the roads were like ice. Luckily we had roughed a good many horses. It was blowing a blizzard and, of course, everyone walked, except the drivers, who put blankets over their shoulders. The men and the horses were continually falling. The wagons were soon covered in snow. There were three miles of troops in front of us, and vehicles were continually getting stuck. All along there were wagons over, with men hauling and the poor horses being whipped. It reminded me of a picture of the retreat from Moscow. It got so bad that we seldom went more than a hundred yards without a stop. After seven hours' hard-going we had only done five miles! It was freezing harder than ever, and was getting dark. I walked at the rear of the Battery and had the job of starting off all our wagons that got stuck. Down a hill, one of the wheel horses fell, but luckily the breeching stopped it being run over by the gun limbers; it merely slid along the icy surface for about twenty yards. The ice was now about one inch thick all over the road. I noticed that one of my knees had swelled up like a cricket ball as the result of a fall, and wondered what it would be like by the end of the journey.

Then we had the job of moving through a town. We had horses down in every single one of our fifteen teams, and had to spread blankets on the road to help them get up. At these continual halts we had to go round kicking up fellows who had dropped to sleep by the wayside and, in case they froze, make them keep walking up and down. One man had got hold of some drink in the town and became so drunk he could not keep on his feet. As he would freeze if we put him on a wagon, we tied his wrists to the rear of the last wagon so that he had to try to walk, although he got dragged along by his wrists each time he fell. It was rough treatment, but he was none the worse for it.

No one had anything to eat for fifteen hours. Word came back that we could not reach our destination as the head of the column was baffled by a hill which it was impossible to mount in its icy condition, and we were told to picket on the road for the rest of the night. It was then 2.30 a.m. We had done seven and a half miles in thirteen hours. We commandeered a farm near-by, much to the rage of the farmer [who abused us]. Tea was made, and we all lay down in a barn half full of straw for a couple of hours. We then had to dig the harness out of the snow and were on the march by seven. To my surprise, the swelling on my knee had completely disappeared.

We marched in Batteries independently, so were able to pass many troops and got to our billet at 1 p.m. It was a lovely chateau which had been occupied by the French. Spring beds and sheets—horses under cover, and Persian carpets. Monsieur le Comte was there also. We stayed there one day, then came up here into action. It is a lovely town. My brother [Harold] is not old but rather an ass to drop his aitches. [Arras.] We were invited to dine with the officers of the French Battery and had a gorgeous spread in a tunnel under a railway embankment— eight course dinner with a variety of wines and we toasted each other in champagne.

The next morning we took over from the French Battery. They showed us their 75s and fired a dozen rounds for our benefit. We were green with envy as, with their wonderful buffers, there was hardly any recoil. They could fire five rounds in succession without relaying, and so are able to fire at about three times the speed we can. In addition to their commissioned officers, they had two cadet officers called 'Aspirants'—nice young fellows.

In the afternoon, Monsieur le Capitaine took the Captain and me to their O.P. to show us the sector. It was very funny, because Monsieur le Capitaine liked to talk in English (rather badly!), while our Captain insisted on talking in French, so they retaliated by saying they could not understand what the other was saying.

At the O.P. there was only one peep hole. Monsieur le

Capitaine looked through first, trying to describe the salient points, saying, 'You see that so and so', and the Captain would reply in French that he could not see it. Then the Captain examined the sector through the peep hole, and he, without thinking, would say, 'You see that so and so'. Monsieur le Capitaine would reply, 'Excuse, I do not see'. They then both burst out laughing and shook hands. I nearly upset the *entente cordiale* in the morning when they had been trying to set our guns for us, by saying under my breath to the Captain. 'That's no darned good.' He gave me a sharp dig in the ribs and I pretended to stumble over a stone, but saw out of the corner of my eye Monsieur le Capitaine looking suspiciously at me.

Then, in the afternoon, I joined the signallers in the cellar of the O.P. where they were having drinks of wine offered by the French signallers and were toasting everything they could think of. One of ours, a Cockney, jokingly said, *'Vive le Bosch'*. The French were just about to drink, when the forms of their visages suddenly changed. I quickly tapped my head and pointed to the Cockney with a laugh. He laughed and they all laughed, and started slapping each other on the back in great camaraderie.

We fight in peace here and live in a most wonderful chateau with porcelain bath and hot and cold water laid on. How quiet compared with Tom's Dog. Hardly a shot fired. We will be having to get mess dress soon! I hope it will liven up a bit as the war will never end at this rate.

The dugouts are twenty feet deep. Everything is most luxurious. Even the sergeants have separate rooms with spring beds. Of course, all the men have beds and sofas and pianos, etc. On the way to the O.P. there are many shops where we can buy fresh fish, watches, groceries, etc., and even a photographer! Herewith a sample of his handiwork. Our guns are comfortably ensconced in a nice position behind our chateau and actually fire over it, as the chateau lies in a hollow.

It is odd to hear the Battery suddenly open up while lying in one's bath in the morning and I wonder what the chap at the O.P. has spotted.

With private stables for our chargers and the garden of fruit and vegetables being looked after for our comfort by a French gardener left by the owner of the place, we feel as if we have arrived in a sort of wonderland.

We are having perfectly glorious weather now. The violets in the garden are lovely and the goldfish in the pond come to the top to sun themselves. You can picture us war-wracked fellows now undergoing our daily hardships of awakening to the songs of nightingales and coming down to breakfast of porridge, bacon and eggs, and coffee, at a great mahogany table with the scent of the pines wafting through the open windows.

The C.R.A. came round with some Indian Rajah to inspect our Battery. The men paraded behind their gun pits. With the party was an old fellow called Sally Dunwater, who was a great athlete and was up at Cambridge with you. He is on the staff as an A.D.C. and has just come from Egypt where he met Uncle Julian. He was wildly delighted to hear I was your son and kept pumping my hand up and down much to the amusement of the Rajah, the General and the men.

I dined last week with the Infantry at Battalion Headquarters. They are Cousin Harry's regiment. I do so enjoy my visits to them, they are such a very nice lot. At dinner all the courtesies and the ritual with the port, etc., are observed, but all so natural and gay. Old Colonel Green said he saw me on leave walking down Piccadilly with a young lady (that must have been [cousin] Nata, although, of course, he did not know it) so naturally I got ragged about it. He said he thought of digging me in the ribs with his walking stick, but decided not to, as I might have been angry at thus being interrupted! He is such a jolly old fellow with his merry red face and twinkle in his eye.

I rode down to the wagon lines yesterday and had a lovely gallop. The drivers are revelling in this summer weather and are taking great pride in their harness. It is hung out near the roadside so that all who pass can admire it, and it really does look rather beautiful with all the links of the chains gleaming like silver.

This morning I spent several hours strengthening the O.P. and rigging up a speaking tube from the post in the roof to the telephone post in the cellar. It is very much like a Heath Robinson picture, as it is rigged up with any old drainpipes and waterpipes I could lay hands on. The joints are tied up with old bits of curtains and a paraffin tin with the bottom knocked out for one end and a tin bucket at the other to shout into.

Duffin of C Battery invited me to lunch at his O.P., which is a similar sort of battered building to ours, just across the road. On going along, I saw him jumping up and down on a board at the entrance and asked him what he was doing. He said he was trying to make our lunch tender. He lifted the board, and there was the steak! We toasted it, and it was very good.

Last week the Captain came round with me to see where we could get good views of the German lines. We came across a very large ruin without a wall standing, and underneath was a most wonderful system of cellars. Regular catacombs, where it would be quite possible to lose oneself, and there are cellars again underneath. The whole town seems to be quite riddled with underground passages.

During my last visit to the O.P., a German heavy Battery fired forty shells just in front of us, of which all but five failed to explode. By the merest chance I spotted the Battery while looking through the telescope at a farmhouse about five thousand yards off, where I noticed six men walking about and then saw a puff of smoke. We got a heavy Battery onto it next day. Last night I had dinner with the Infantry and then went round with Captain Frewen hunting for bomb guns. They pitched about thirty bombs over when we were there, and I was able to spot four different guns. With luck we will knock them out tomorrow.

It is still very quiet here with still the same old rigmarole every day. Our thoughts and talk centre round our particular job and piece of the line, such as the strength and direction of the wind and its effect on the angles and ranges, or what telephone lines should be laid, or what small parties of Germans we saw from the O.P., or what effect our fire had on them, etc. There is not enough exercise. Men of fifty could do the work we are doing. I have just fixed a trapeze from a tall tree near the Battery where it is possible to swing thirty feet into the air either way.

To liven things up, I bought some iodine crystals and a small bottle of ammonia from the chemist on the way back from the O.P., and made some small pills which, when dry, go off with loud bangs (as we used to do at school). Lennox was sitting in the mess near the fire. I put a pill on the hearth-stone and warned him of the bang. He did not believe it and took the bellows. When he blew it, it went off with such a bang that he fell over backwards. I left the rest of the stuff in an egg-cup on the mantelpiece. When the Captain came in later, he sat by the fire and started to read a book. While reading he reached up for his matches with his right hand, and put two of his fingers in the egg-cup. He made an exclamation and I saw his fingers covered with the stuff, so told him he should wash quickly or he might have one of his nails blown off. He looked surprised so I threw a pill into the fire and it went off with a bang. He was NOT amused, but went off to wash.

APRIL FOOL

I am at present in command of the Battery, as the Captain has gone on leave. Only for ten days, thank goodness, as the amount of orders I have to plough through every day is something prodigious (about twenty-five foolscap sheets), but otherwise life is varied with most of my time spent away from the Battery, either at the wagon lines, O.P., or Infantry.

The very second day after he left, I was nearly up for court martial. It happened like this.

At about 5 on a dreary, drizzly morning, when I was at the O.P., I suddenly realized it was 1 April, so thought of a ruse to get the Adjutant out of bed by sending him word of a juicy target on a bogus map reference that sounded like part of our sector. After a moment's thought, I called to the signallers below to send this message to Brigade: 'Can you get heavies to fire on armoured train derailed at X38 central'. (For X I gave the letter which comprised the part of the sector we covered, but which, like other alphabetical squares, does not have more than thirty-six numbered squares.)

Unless he was very wide awake, he would jump out of bed and try to look up the reference on his map and so become an April fool. Instead of this, he passed the message straight through to Divisional Headquarters, where our Brigade Major, who is a bit of a fire-eater, rang up our Heavy Artillery to engage the target forthwith. They stood to, I heard afterwards, for nearly an hour in the rain, ready to fire, while their officers puzzled over the map reference and asked for verification of the square's number, etc. When at last maps had been well and truly checked, and it was finally realized that there was no such square, the fun began, and back came the boomerang first to the Brigade-Major, who, fuming with rage, called up the Brigade for an explanation.

The first I knew about it was a wrathful call from the Colonel himself, demanding an explanation. He finally ended with, 'Did you see an armoured train?' When I replied, 'No, Sir,' he shouted, 'What the hell do you mean by it? I am coming to see you!' When he arrived I was surprised to see our C.R.A. with him. Expecting a fearful dressing-down, I was nonplussed when the General was as genial as could be and wished me to show him the whole sector our guns were covering. He thanked me and, when he went out, the Colonel turned to me saying, 'Now, what is the meaning of all this?' All I could reply, and very submissively, was that it was 1 April. He sort of exploded at this and rushed out, saying over his shoulder, 'You should not make a fool of Army matters'.

An hour or so afterwards, I got a phone call from Lennox at the Battery saying somewhat diffidently, 'I have just had orders to put you under arrest,' to which I asked, 'Open or close arrest?' He seemed a bit confused at this, and then said, 'Open,' to which I replied, 'Then I shall continue to command the Battery'.

It began to dawn on me later that Lennox had been trying to pull my leg. Anyway, when Chadwick came to relieve me, I went down to the Infantry and told Colonel Green what had happened. He slapped his knee with delight and just roared with laughter. When he recovered, he said, 'If there is to be a court martial, I will be your "prisoner's friend",' and he made me have a sherry with him. I was never very anxious about the outcome of a court martial, if there was to be one, because, since the map reference did not exist, no ammunition could have been fruitlessly expended. And what is more, it showed that the staff folk were a bit hazy about their maps!

The news of the episode spread like wildfire. When I rode to the wagon lines seven miles off, they had already heard of it. I was kept informed of the latest news from Divisional Headquarters by officers coming from there. The confusion there was fearful, but they all knew now that it was an April fool, except the Brigade Major, and they were not going to tell him for fear of hurting his feelings! Luckily for me, the General (who was not turned out of bed) was said to be highly amused. I cannot go anywhere now without hilarious illusions to the leg pull, but I am going to keep well clear of the Heavy Battery!

I was up a tree last night. It was a large fir tree in front of the O.P. and about 600 yards from the enemy lines. Some of its branches spoilt the view. The branches started about thirty feet up. We had a 15 foot ladder, so I had to swarm up the last bit, with a saw and billhook round my neck. I had to wait a while, because the moon was too bright. About 2 a.m., it started to rain and was dark enough to start operations. The saw was awful, the teeth not even set, so I had to get to work with the billhook. It seemed to make a fearful noise in that quiet night, and I thought the Bosch might hear me. Anyway, it occurred to me that if they did spot me I was in the right place, because below me was the cemetery. No bullets came my way, however, and by 3.30 the job was finished, and by 4 a.m. I was back at the O.P., when it was just getting light enough to spy out the land with the telescope. On being relieved I had to go on to the Infantry in my thoroughly filthy state, which caused much light-hearted conjecture as to my nocturnal activities.

A few days ago, who should turn up at the O.P. but Arthur Hamilton, who had cycled over from his Division to see me. He had called at the Battery and was given an orderly to show him up. He was much taken with our little observing den, with its maps and flash spotter, etc. I only had some bread and cheese which we took to the cellar where the signallers worked, and toasted it over a fire. At four, we walked back to our chateau. He was very surprised at the splendour in which we lived. He wanted to return after tea, but one of my orderlies had gone off on his bike with a message, so he had to stay for dinner. After tea I showed him the sights and introduced him to a vast gun on a mighty platform which had sprung up near-by, but we were shooed off by a sentry for daring to look on such a sacred object.

It continues to be quiet here, but two days ago it was quite like old times for a few minutes. I was walking along the pavement of one of the streets, which had a high wall on the other side, when the Huns started a strafe. Suddenly a shell came through the wall making a hole about ten feet in diameter and landed in the middle of the road. I tried to dive into the pavement with my feet towards the shell. All the stones, etc., whizzed over me, hitting the wall above my head which I had covered with my hands, and dropped harmlessly about and on top of me, so I escaped with a couple of bruises. I was pleased to note that my reflexes in dodging danger were still active! The annoying part was that I tore my breeches at the knee and spoilt them.

With all this inaction we get pestered with silly details, such as being called upon for a statement as to whether the grease for the wheels was inferior to that which we were usually issued with, or cursed because Driver so-and-so had an odd pair of spurs on, etc. The men complained the other day about their rations —tins of pork and beans had been issued in place of bully. It was not enough and no pork was visible. I reported this, and the reply came that the complaint was not understood since the food value was the same as the bully and that the pork was absorbed in beans! I wrote back saying this was no comfort and that one might just as well issue the men with meat lozenges on this theory. Anyhow, it was agreed that when pork and beans was issued thereafter, the men had half a tin of bully as well.

One Q.M.G. fellow had a sense of humour, because, when we indent for replacements, we have to give reasons for the loss and invariably put 'destroyed by shell fire'. Two of our chaps happened to have lost their identity discs (which, of course, are supposed always to be worn round the neck on a string). I added these to the list and back came the remark with the new discs, that these men had evidently had remarkable escapes!

Last Wednesday we had a great boxing tournament. The referee was a subaltern named Ellison in B Battery. He had been champion lightweight in Alaska. We had a friendly go the other day when he gave me some useful hints. He is an amusing chap. He spent five years bear hunting, trapping and goldmining in Alaska and North Canada and has a fund of stories.

One day, as I was approaching his Battery, a shell hit the officers' latrine, sending the screen flying. I was shocked to see a man left sitting there on the throne and thought he must be dead. I ran as hard as I could, and arrived to find Ellison up and adjusting his trousers. He said with a grin, 'It was lucky that shell came when it did as I was feeling a bit constipated!'

Cavanagh rang me up last Friday to say that my April fool had got to the ears of the Army Commander and, being a stuffy old beast, he had ordered a court of inquiry with the Colonel as President. The Court was to sit at Brigade Headquarters at 11 next morning. In some trepidation, I went round all booted and spurred to be welcomed by Cavanagh in great glee, saying, 'Ah!

Hot Stuff [his nickname for me], just in time to join us in a drink', to the merriment of the others. So he got his own back all right, and was still more delighted when I told him how I had been wondering which was worse, to be cashiered or dismissed from the service. Anyway, we had quite a good party with the Colonel as always his kindly cheerful self.

An elderly captain from Colonel Green's Battalion, which we are covering, has been staying with us for four days as representative of his Battalion, to get an insight into our work. His name is Rixon [he later won the M.C., rose to rank of Colonel, but, later in the war, was killed]. He is Rixon of Fort Rixon in Rhodesia and went through the Matabele War with Uncle Teddie [who hoisted the Flag at Fort Salisbury in 1890]. They were both in charge of artillery units in those days so naturally he was most interested to have news of him.

Did I tell you Dobbie was wounded? He got a blighty one about three weeks ago with some pieces of H.E. shell.

CHAPTER 10

Still at Arras

It is nearly three months now since we left Tom's Dog. We are gradually making Sundays a bit of a change for the men at the gun lines. There are no fatigues and 25 per cent of the men (as that is all we can spare) attend Church Parade at 10 a.m. In the afternoon, some hot baths have been put at our disposal and we can send off 25 per cent at a time. We have found some rhubarb growing nearby so there is stewed rhubarb for tea. After that, there is football and boxing, making it quite a good day. The men play football against other batteries on a pitch about 300 yards away. It has two large crump holes on it about five feet deep, and it is quite a funny sight when two or three players plunge into them to try to get the ball.

We celebrated the anniversary of our arrival in France last Saturday by having a footer match with C Battery. We played them both up here and down at the wagon lines, and beat them at both places. We procured a barrel of beer for each place, also cakes. In the evening, we had a singsong where each of us subs had to sing. Pretty rotten songs they were, but greeted with vociferous cheers. The only song I could remember was one I had heard at our O.T.C. camp: 'Why did Whaley swallow JoJo'. Duffin laughed so much that he fell off his chair. We also fired a salvo at a target at ultimate range, which was really off our sector, and instead of giving 'retaliation' or 'registration', etc., as the reason in our report, we just put, 'jubilation'.

We were having drinks yesterday with Gunning in his motor lorry to celebrate his command of a trench mortar battery (the mortars look like footballs with sticks attached that you drop down the spout of portable gunlets and they spew them out over the German trenches), when one of our planes, which had obviously been hit, came rushing in and managed to land on the race course just opposite. As it was obvious that the German guns would open up on it, Gunning raced off in his lorry and reached the plane just as the shelling started, got the pilot out, who had been hit in the shoulder, and was away, a second before the plane had a direct hit and burst into flames. It was quite a fine spectacle. When he got back, we all drank his health and that of the pilot who seemed in good spirits.

Lennox has left to finish his medical course in Edinburgh, so I am the only one left of the officers who came out with the Battery. He has been replaced by a fellow just out of the Shop, named Gifford. A nice young fellow. I can call him this as he is actually a few months younger than I am.

Then, last week, news of my regular commission came through, but only as Second Lieutenant.

The Captain told me how upset the General was that his recommendation had not been accepted. I thought I would now become the junior subaltern in the Battery. However, next day an order was published saying that I was to retain my seniority while serving with the Division.

The Captain and I went down to the remains of a village [Blangy] through which both ours and the enemy trenches run.

It is a most extraordinary mix-up, since, in places, the trenches are so close that they run through the remains of the same houses. In consequence, nobody thinks of throwing grenades about—a case of 'those who live in glass houses . . .'. Wanting to find vantage points where we could see the lie of the land on the enemy side, we went up into the roof of a part of a house that was still standing and which we thought was about 100 yards from the enemy's lines. Most of the tiles were missing, and as we were looking through the rafters the Captain touched me and pointed to our left. There we were, looking down on German trenches a few yards away and saw some Germans standing there. I gasped and whispered: 'Why don't they shoot us?' 'I can't think,' said he with a grin, but we crept softly away.

The Captain sent me down to the wagon lines last week to see that all was shipshape for the General's inspection the following day. I was up early in order to get there in time to see the horses watered, groomed and fed, and inspected the harness, which was gleaming.

The inspection, which went off satisfactorily, was over by 11.30, so I jumped on my horse and was back at the gun lines by lunchtime, and went up to the O.P. in the afternoon. That night, I went down with a gunner to the remains of an iron foundry, which is about 400 yards from the Hun lines and very much battered about, to see if there was anything useful lying about there. We found a splendid anvil, but it weighed over four hundredweight. We had to move it to the road 150 yards off. There happened to be a pair of old truck wheels and we managed to balance the anvil on these, and get it to the road after about three-quarters of an hour's work.

Best of all, we found a portable forge. I never expected such luck. It had been hit in five different places, but the bellows were all right, so we hauled it, too, along to the road. We also found a vice, weighing nearly two hundredweight, and a chain with three pulleys. We then went off to get three more men and a cart. The cart made a fearful noise, rumbling along the cobbled road, and we eventually got stuck at a barrier. The Bosch, hearing us stop, guessed we had got stuck and started shooting, but shot at the wrong barrier. Ha! Ha!

With great struggles and puffings, we got the things on board. It was raining hard by then, so, filthy with rust and sopping wet, we arrived triumphantly back with the spoils. All these precious items are now installed at the wagon lines, much to the delight of the Farrier Sergeant, who has been limited to cold-shoeing ever since we have been out. Now all the horses will be really well shod for a change and, out of the kindness of our hearts, we are going to allow the other batteries to use our forge!

It is curious how everyone in England seems to feel the loss of Lord Kitchener. It has not had the slightest effect on the troops out here. We had all felt that his work was really over before the news of his death came along. We regarded him more as a political figurehead and representative of the Army to Foreign Powers. I think people in England were apt to idolize him a bit, and did not realize that practically all the work and responsibility was being borne by others at the time of his death.

Parry brought me news last month that I could go on leave, but I felt rather awful about it, because several of my men with wives and families had not had leave at all. During the time we have been out here together, quite a number of them have brought me snapshots of their wives and kids, when they received them in the post. I never quite know what to say except, 'Fine little chaps,' or similar sounds of admiration. So I told Parry I would prefer to wait until the strawberry season was in full blast in England. A fortnight later all leave was cancelled. Parry brought me this news, saying with a grin, 'Serves you right, you greedy gut!'

You know, the trouble out here is that I am having too good a time. All you people are thinking we are fighting for King and country, etc., etc., while we are sitting here eating strawberries (the chateau garden is full of them just now) or working off bilious attacks from over-eating! It puts one in a false position.

We had an elderly Captain staying with us here for a few days (the War Office sends out officers from Home Divisions on Cook's Tours to get some idea of what active service is like). He wrote us such a nice letter thanking us for our hospitality, and said the only thing he had to complain of was that his sleep was occasionally disturbed by the songs of the nightingales! Since he left, however, a stray whizz-bang actually did hit our chateau, just above the upstairs bathroom, showering the place with plaster and brick dust. I was shaving at the time and was so startled that I nearly cut myself!

We had two Cook's tourists sent out to us when we were in the Ypres salient. One had been a schoolmaster—quite a decent fellow, but on his third day, while ducking from some shells, a splinter hit him on his seat. He was not badly hurt, but had to be sent home—rather ignominious for him. The other tended to throw his weight about a bit and said he wanted to see some real strafing. A few hours later, the enemy obliged and gave the Battery quite a pasting. Our Cook's tourist, looking rather pale, came along and said he wished to go and see how things were down at our wagon lines. It was the last we saw of him!

The papers are full of good news. They say that the offensive has only just started, so I think that after a month or so, the Hun will begin to get a bit tired of it. I see from the papers that Warwickshire is a good place from which to hear the guns on the Somme. We hear them pretty well from here. They sound like a convoy of drays rattling under a railway bridge on a cobbled road—rumble, rumble, rumble.

I have rigged up a cold bath at the O.P. out of a large tank; it is splendid to break the monotony of staring through a telescope by having a bath every now and then. Yesterday, I suddenly had orders to fire while having one, so had to dash upstairs and carry on operations in a towel.

We had a conference last week at Brigade H.Q. of all battery commanders and senior subalterns, to discuss the difficulties to be expected in the event of an advance. The Colonel was in the chair, and we all sat round. When the Colonel put the question, Cavanagh jumped up saying, 'Well, Sir, one of the difficulties to be faced, but by no means the only one, will be the possible resistance put up by the enemy!' The Colonel told him to try to be serious. I suggested bullet-proof tubes of ten feet diameter with hand rails inside, holding about ten men, who would use the rails as a treadmill and so roll the tubes over the trenches and barbed wire. After a long and very lighthearted discussion at which all sorts of ideas were aired, it was decided that each battery should have a portable wooden bridge to enable it to cross trenches. Everyone seemed to be in high spirits at the thought that we might be on the move at last.

We might have the chance of some open fighting for a change, when our gunners would have the satisfaction of seeing the effect of their shooting. Gifford became quite lyrical when I told him the news, and said, 'Just to think of repelling a charge using fuse zero, with every gun spewing out its 365 round metal balls like mammoth shot guns.' I must say it does sound rather exhilarating.

It is a simply glorious day today. I was just thinking of this day last year—so different from the peace and boredom of today—the day of the liquid fire attack.

CHAPTER 11

The Somme

Of all the queer places to find oneself, here I am in bed in Somerville College for young ladies, in Oxford. The Undergraduates have been moved to Oriel.

I thought you might like to hear of my doings since we left Arras, although it is a rather long-winded affair and all about myself.

On the last day of July [1916], greatly to our joy, we at last had orders that we were to be relieved on a certain night. We pulled out half a Battery at a time, after handing over to the incoming Battery. I took out the first half and reached the wagon lines at 3 a.m. We were up at 6 a.m., working hard all day beginning to make ready for the move. Next night, the rest of the Battery arrived at 2 a.m. and we started our march at 3 a.m. reaching our first camping ground at 11 a.m. Throughout the whole march to the Somme, we were blessed with the most glorious weather, and health flowed into everyone in leaps and bounds. All the flabby anaemic faces became hard and sunburnt.

On the way, while walking on foot, I saw what looked like a General coming our way, and said to Chadwick, 'Who is that old buffer?' When he reached us, and we had saluted, he glared at me for a moment, and then said, 'Well, young fellow, been pulling anyone's leg lately?' He was General Cowper, our Divisional Commander!

When we were nearing the concentration area, I was sent forward on a bicycle to find our field and to mark out the lines for our horses and guns, etc. It was very hot and dusty. I passed thousands of troops and reached the area where there were simply acres of cavalry. It was then 3 p.m. and, as I had had nothing since breakfast, I was feeling a bit done in, when Gunning hailed me from his covered wagon and invited me in. He gave me a stiff whisky to buck me up, but it went straight to my head. I told him he must help me by taking me to the picketing site, where he linked arms with me as I could not walk straight! Together we went round, marking out the lines and by the time we had finished I was all right, and so escaped the awful calamity of being found drunk on duty!

During our march, our strength of subalterns was increased by one per battery; we were joined by a Canadian called Nodder.

From there we moved on next morning, and halted some miles behind the lines, then the Colonel and Battery Commanders and some of us subalterns went up to reconnoitre. During the night, the Batteries came up and took over from another Brigade. Our position was bad and in view of the enemy. The O.P. was also bad. The Captain and I found a better place, though rather unhealthy both because of the shelling and the large number of corpses about. Then we strolled down to the trenches towards High Wood, to see what could be seen from there. It reminded me of Ypres, only a bit more lively. We had to fire continuously night and day, about a thousand rounds every twenty-four hours. It was very tiring as the guns were really on their last legs; they had to be pushed back after each round because the recoil buffers no longer functioned properly. The rifling in the guns had become so worn that we had to calibrate them and adjust errors in their ranges, by adding so many yards to the ranges given, for each particular gun.

After four days, we moved our position about 800 yards to our right, to a much better spot some 80 yards behind a shallow crest, and only 1,400 yards from the enemy trenches. We had to cross a trench just behind our new position, so we borrowed a bridge from B Battery, much to their disgust. These bridges were heavy, cumbersome things, and we had conveniently left ours behind. B Battery had carried theirs all the way from Arras, only to lend it to us!

We had to find new O.Ps. All the land around had been completely ploughed up by shell fire. Craters touching in every direction. We found a good spot in the lip of a crater, but the smell was pretty powerful from the rotting bodies: it was rather grizzly, and heart-rending, seeing them blackened in the sun, with their white teeth showing. They were the remains of a trench mortar team, and, from the way that they were spread-eagled, the shell must have burst right in their midst.

We were not certain of our exact position, but while looking through my field-glasses, lying on my tummy, my elbow felt something hard. On scratching the earth away, we saw a large bit of millstone. There, on our map, was marked a windmill, so we could fix our position exactly. Further to our right were the very shattered remains of Longueval and Delville Wood where the stumps of a few trees were still standing. We found a wonderful spot at Longueval in the remains of a cellar of what once had been a house. From there, we could see right up the length of the enemy trenches running up to High Wood, and could even see German sentries in them. Of course, the Bosch knew that there must be good vantage points hereabouts, and kept pasting unceasingly.

Never have I seen so many bloated flies. They were so thick in our dugouts that we lit fires with newspapers on going in, then they just fell in clouds to the ground.

One evening, when Nodder and I were discussing the ammunition position with Sergeant Bliss and the Battery Clerk during a short lull, there was a burst of shrapnel about twenty yards above us. We had become so used to these things that we merely inclined our heads towards the burst, so that our tin hats would take the odd bullet, and I was about to continue when Nodder exclaimed, 'I am hit,' and fell. I saw a small hole in his chest on opening his coat, and, on looking round, saw Sergeant Bliss tending the Battery Clerk, who was also stretched out. They both died within a minute—very sad—they only had one bullet each.

Some more shrapnel burst near while we were tending them, but without effect.

When the ammunition supplies came up that night we had, as usual, to report casualties. I could find no casualty return forms, so had to use the forms for equipment. It seemed cold-blooded, indenting for a subaltern and battery clerk, to replace those 'destroyed by shell fire'.

There were only two of us subalterns left by now, and the Captain nearly went also that night: he was standing in front of one of our guns when it fired. I saw him lit up by the flash, standing there with his walking stick. He walked slowly round as if nothing had happened. He is a remarkable man.

The next evening Captain Boscawan of the 60th came through our Battery with his company on their way to the trenches. When they were about twenty yards in front of the guns, just to give him a bit of a fright, I shouted, 'Battery Action'. You should have seen the look on his face as he swung round and then when he saw the grin on my face, he shook his stick at me.

A day or two later, we had orders to cut the German wire. The Captain went down for the first half of the day, and I did the second half. It was ticklish work, since our guns were so close that the shells, to be effective, had to burst about three yards above our heads. The two signallers and I were in a front sap which had been cleared of Infantry as there were bound to be some short bursts which might spray the place. Later on, the Infantry came into the sap, and so, to avoid casualties, I had to change to H.E. that only burst on impact. It was not so effective in cutting the wire, blowing it up and knocking it down again. All went well for a bit. Beautiful bursts right into the wire. The signaller each time reported, 'Battery fired', and the next moment—bang—and up went the wire. We could not hear the shells coming because, with the very short range, they travelled faster than sound. Suddenly, with the next salvo, I was caught in the back with a clod of earth and thought one of our shells had burst short. We were about to continue when, to my surprise, I saw at my feet the shell lying unexploded and said to the signaller, 'Look!' His eyes nearly popped out. It had apparently hit the ground behind and hurtled on base, first, hitting the parapet, after ripping my gas helmet from my side, and dropped into the trench. After taking the marking of the defective shell, we heaved it over the parapet so that none of the Infantry would see it.

When we returned that evening, the enemy had been soaking the rear trenches with tear gas. Without my gasmask I arrived back with streaming eyes, and feeling as if I had a fearful cold in the head, but it soon wore off.

On the evening of the 17th, we received word that our attack would take place the following day at 3 p.m.—an odd time to choose, we thought. The Captain told me that I and another subaltern had been picked to be F.O.O.s for two Brigades concentrated on that sector. The other fellow was to stay at Battalion H.Q. and be responsible for sending back all the information, and I was to go over with the Infantry and do what I thought best as the occasion arose. The prospect of directing the fire of thirty-two guns was rather thrilling. I was on duty with the Battery until 2 a.m., then, as the odds were against my returning next day, I told my batman what to do with my kit should I not return and then went to sleep till 5 a.m.

When I was starting down in full warpaint—to wit, pockets full of biscuits and raisins—the Captain came to wish me luck and said, 'Remember, the longer you can remain alive the greater use you will be'. I promised to do my best about this, and went off with two signallers, Edwards and Moss, who had asked to come with me—both wonderful chaps. They carried half a mile of wire, and the signallers' flags. On reaching the trenches, I arranged with the other subaltern that he should collect information both from the Infantry and from me and pass it on, so that I should be free from sending situation reports and could concentrate on switching the guns onto machine guns and other troublesome targets. I gave the signallers the job of laying two alternative lines from the sap from which we should operate to the Battalion H.Q., and went up twice during the morning to test the lines; I also spent some time trying to detect movements of the enemy during certain concentrations of fire on strong points, but could see nothing.

We got a rough time for a few minutes from our heavies which mistook our front sap for the Bosch lines—quite easy in that mix-up where the trenches had been almost obliterated —and got covered with earth and stuff two or three times. I reported this at once. There were, fortunately, no Infantry there at the time.

Just before the attack the Infantry came up and deployed to the right and left of us, crawling from one shell hole to another. I sent word down to switch on to machine gun posts and the Bosch did not trouble our men as they crept forward.

Exactly at 1500 hours, our guns put up a most perfect fire on the enemy less than one hundred yards ahead, and dozens of Bosches jumped up and ran, zig-zagging like rabbits. I got so excited that I picked up a rifle and had some pot shots, as the Infantry were doing, and saw several bowled over. As our bombardment on that line was to last only three minutes, I got fearfully worried because our men were not moving forward fast enough, knowing that as soon as our fire lifted, the enemy machine guns would pop up and mow them down. I did what I could to get them to get a move on, but without much result. When our guns lifted, up popped the machine guns, with our men only half-way across, and several stout Germans, standing waist high, poured fire on them, thus holding up the whole attack. Some twenty men of the second wave who were near us, started picking them off. It was an extraordinary sight, with an incredible din of machine gun fire that sounded almost solid. Among so much that happened all at once was the sight of a man running forward and suddenly throwing up his hands with a rifle in one of them—I had seen a spurt of dust come out of the back of his pack. It reminded me of a picture of the Boer War. Several of our men lying in shell holes were throwing their tin hats high into the air.

With the enemy going full blast with their machine guns,

the only thing to do was to try to get our guns back again. My communications were all broken by then, and the only thing I could think of was an old petrol tin that marked the end of the sap, about half way to the Bosch lines. This I stuck on the bayonet at the end of a rifle, and with this, signalled back in Morse, lifting it up and down, hoping it would be seen by the other F.O.O. I only got the word 'Drop' out before the tin was shot away. Edwards then tried a flag. At last, after what seemed a long time, perhaps five minutes, our guns dropped back again, and the machine-gunning almost ceased. As we were so close to the German lines, some of our shrapnel could not help spraying us.

While I was standing watching the effect of our fire, I suddenly found myself in a sort of dream and remember thinking, 'This is extraordinary, as I thought we were having a battle'. Then it occurred to me that perhaps I had been shot, and felt myself sinking away and thought, 'Ah! I am a gonner'. Soon the sinking stopped and I thought, 'Ah! I am not a gonner'. (You know, it has since made me think that the nicest way to be executed would be by a firing squad. One would only hear the 'Ready, Present, Fi' and then be in dreamland—no sound of the bang, just a feeling of gently sinking away.)

Later, I found myself lying in the shell hole with my legs crumpled up underneath me and with my thumb between my teeth. I heard one of the signallers, who was bending over me, saying, 'Oh! he is hit in the mouth', and had a terrible thought that he would push a field dressing down my throat. The only thing I could do was to glare at him. Suddenly, feeling came back, and the wind at the same time, and it was just as if I had been kicked by a horse in the back. Gradually feeling came back to my legs, then I started to breathe, which hurt so much that I tried not to. The signallers had found a round hole in my left shoulder-blade, and poured in some iodine and put on a field dressing. As all the stretchers were in use for worse cases, my signallers helped me to walk about 300 yards back to an aid post, and then went to report to Perrin, the other

F.O.O. There I sat for a bit, propped against the wall of the trench, but as one of the orderlies swung back, squashing my head against the wall with his backside whenever a shell fell close, I decided to move on and got as far as Battalion H.Q.; there, I was met by Perrin.

It was just getting dark when, after a short rest, Perrin took my right wrist and led me along a trench for nearly half a mile. It was rough-going, as the enemy set up a heavy bombardment trying to catch reinforcements. We had to drop flat several times, and the exertion caused me to cough up some blood. After a wait of an hour or so, a stretcher arrived, and, by then, I had found how to ease the breathing—by taking very tiny breaths of about a spoonful at a time—and could talk, after a fashion.

The two stretcher bearers carried me a long way and as they seemed to be puffing and blowing a lot, I asked them what the fuss was about as I only weighed nine stone. To which one said, 'Sure you ain't got a bit of Jack Johnson inside yer?'

It was dark on arrival at the dressing station where I was laid on the ground. There was a light drizzle which was comforting. I was relieved of my wristwatch and field-boots, and thought how kind people were. There were dozens of wounded lying around. After some hours, I was taken in for attention. There was a delightful doctor who said the Colonel had asked for news of me, which cheered me up. He told me I would have an injection. I thought this would be for tetanus and was not looking forward to it, as I had heard they pump about a tumblerful in, and it hurts more than the wound. However, it was only morphia and I was then put on one side with a label round my neck marked 'Not to be Moved'. The pain of breathing went, and I felt wonderfully comfortable.

Next morning, four of us were put in an ambulance and off we went at great speed, bumping over ruts and shell holes. We had to hold on to stop ourselves from falling out of our bunks. This was the worst experience of all. One of the others, who had been shot in the head, was screaming most of the way, and when we were pulled out at a rear dressing station he was dead, poor chap.

We went on in another ambulance and at last arrived at the casualty clearing station where we were put into beds in a large marquee. There were about twenty of us, and the noise of groans was fairly continuous. I was glad of this, because I found groaning eased my breathing and I was able to do so without attracting attention. There was a wonderful sister looking after us at night. She seemed almost unreal, so gentle and sweet, in all that bedlam. Fellows calling out in their delirium. One shouted, 'Charge!' at the top of his voice. It was rather entertaining in a sort of way. The fellow next to me had been shot in the stomach and kept calling for water every few minutes. Eventually he was allowed to have as much as he wanted. This eased him, and he died about an hour later.

Once an orderly, in trying to move me, pulled me by my injured shoulder, which made me swear at him. Later on, that dear sister came over to make me comfortable, and said with a smile, 'I hope I won't deserve the names you called the orderly!'

There was some speculation about where the bullet was inside me. I suggested that it might be near the bottom of my spine as I felt a hard lump there about the size of a shrapnel bullet, but the doctor poo-poohed this. He thought it might have ricocheted off the inside of some ribs which were broken.

As soon as we were fit to travel we were sent to the base. They would not let me go until I had been twenty-four hours without coughing blood. Three days later, after coughing out something that looked like a hunk of raw liver, which seemed to stop the coughing, I was allowed to go. We went in an ambulance train, where I had my first proper sleep, and were taken to a Red Cross hospital in Rouen—the most beautiful one in France, where we were thoroughly spoilt. As I was being taken in, a man in a white coat said 'Hello!' I thought he must be a painter, and replied, 'Hello to you'. Then, he said, 'What would you like?' and I, thinking he was trying to be funny, replied, 'Beer'. He then turned round to someone and said, 'Give the boy some beer'. It turned out that he was Colonel in Charge! I felt rather ashamed of myself, but he always gave me a broad grin each time he saw me. Colonel Dooner (who gave me my commission) was just leaving with a bit of shrapnel inside him, and we had a long talk.

I was X-rayed for the bullet, but they could not find it, so they X-rayed me again next day over a much greater area, and to their surprise saw it lodged somewhere between the heart and the base of the right lung. I suppose the bullet, after entering my left shoulder-blade, must have hit the ribs and bounded off from there, grazing the inside of the spine before coming to rest where it did. The bang on the spine would account for the temporary paralysis of my legs. I was quite a show piece: Sir James Kingston Fowler, chest specialist to Queen Victoria, came to see me. He tapped me about, and asked how I felt, and when I said, 'All right', he seemed quite surprised.

After two days, we were taken to Havre, where we were handled just like baggage—being taken out of the train and put on trollies, four stretchers to a trolley, with labels round our necks, and trundled off to the ship by a porter, where we were picked up by a crane and landed gently on deck—quite a pleasant experience. It was a lovely ship—the *Asturias*—of about 12,000 tons, holding 2,500 wounded. We sailed on the third day and lay in cots slung from long poles.

Everything was most comfortable except that, with some ten cots slung from one pole, every time one chap moved it shook all the other cots, so we did not get much sleep. A doctor patient who was a walking case lent me a warm dressing-gown, and took me on deck where I was able to have a good look at Hayling Island as we passed it.

On arrival at Southampton, some officious staff officer came round asking where we would like to be sent. I heard one man say 'London', whereupon he was told he would be sent to Manchester. I said 'Guildford', whereupon he said I would go to Oxford. I was just as pleased with this, but was careful not to show my pleasure, in case he sent me somewhere else.

We travelled by special train. There were three tiers of bunks down each side of the carriage. The sister and orderlies were able to move about freely in the centre. On arrival, we were brought here by ambulance. It felt funny, visiting Oxford again, in this manner, travelling through the streets feet first, and then to find oneself in a ladies' college.

CHAPTER 12

Blighty

I have been having a pleasant time in this hospital and was allowed up after the first week or so, when Julie [a cousin] came from Holton in her pony trap and took me out for a drive. As I had arrived in England without any kit, and had nothing but hospital pyjamas to wear, she thoughtfully brought some odd pieces of clothing including an old cardigan of Connie's! It was a lovely outing and we had much to talk about.

I have since hired a fiery steed, of barely twelve hands, and a gig so as to visit friends and relatives. (The doctor told me not to ride a motor bike because it would bump me about too much.)

Yesterday I drove over to Holton for lunch with the Langdale-Smiths and had such a warm welcome from the old folk. Julie was there and sportingly agreed to come with me in my conveyance back to Oxford where we spent a joyous afternoon. I felt quite a swell escorting my beautiful cousin round the town and seeing the admiring glances cast in her direction. A tall infatuated major kept following us around, but we managed to give him the slip and dubbed him 'Mephistopheles', whom he so closely resembled. Last week I called round on old Cousin Dora and asked if she would like to come for a drive in the gig but, after looking at the pony, then at the gig, and then at me, she said she would rather not. Perhaps it was just as well, as I enjoy galloping round Carfex in it.

Three of us occupy one room in this hospital overlooking a lovely lawn. One of them, called McCan, is recovering from typhoid. He happened to remark one morning, as we were sitting up in bed about to have breakfast, that he wished he had a nice wound with a bandage to display. I was pulling his leg about this when he squirted a syphon of soda straight in my face. I threw both my fish balls at him and then my teacup which caught him squarely between the eyes, bursting the cup in pieces. That stopped his squirt, and blood starting trickling down. In rushed two V.A.D.s who mopped and bandaged him up. They did not seem the least annoyed with me about it and thought it rather a joke. I told McCan that he ought to thank me for fulfilling his wish so promptly, but he did not respond. Anyway, I took him out in my gig next day.

Mrs Soames, the mother of my Captain, sent me some beautiful flowers and grapes with a warm invitation to call when I leave hospital. They live in Park Crescent opposite Regent's Park. I also had a letter from the Captain giving news of the Battery saying that so far their position had escaped serious attention from the enemy. He told me of the casualties among the men since I left, fortunately only a few. Among them was Sergeant Sheward who had his left arm shot off below the elbow. It will be sad for him as he was a great boxer. The Captain sent me the addresses of relatives of several of my men whose homes are near London and who hoped I would look them up. He says he has two new subalterns. 'One of them,' he writes, 'ex H.A.C., has, I think, less hair than I have!'

Tommy Cavanagh sent me a short note in his usual vein: 'Dear Hot Stuff, Sorry to hear of your illness, now mind! be very careful not to disgrace us in Oxford. The Colonel is most anxious about this. There is no news here except we hope to have a Hell of a battle, about now!'

A later letter from Gifford sent me the sad news that my batman Moir had been badly wounded. He said that the O.P. is now just beyond the trenches we had been attacking when I got pipped and that the view from there is great,

Just think of sitting up here spotting batteries firing, and singing out 4°30. Right P.S. 53-50 Fire!' Just like old times. Aren't you sorry you aren't here? P.S. I have just had a letter from General Sandys telling me that I have got the M.C. Naturally I am thrilled, but isn't it decent of him to write when he must be so frightfully busy. He says the Division has done splendidly and earned enormous kudos and, what is more, both my signallers, who were with me that day, Gunners Moss and Edwards, have won Military Medals.

After about five weeks, the hospital boarded me and gave me two months' sick leave (the maximum at one go). They let me out on condition I started quietly. On arrival in London I called on the Soameses and was shown into Mr Soames's study where he was sitting crumpled in his chair. He looked up and said with a broken voice, 'We are glad to see you but I am afraid you won't be glad to see us.' He handed me a telegram telling them of the death of their son. This, and the deep pain that showed in his eyes, made mine smart. He took me to his wife who begged me to say with them for lunch. It was an ordeal, but somehow they seemed to get some comfort from the few halting words I could say about their son. On reaching Godalming, where I am staying with Aunt Ethel, I wrote them a long letter. It was easy to open one's heart about their son because he was such a fine soldier and such a friend. I received a touching letter of thanks from dear Mrs Soames pressing me to come to see them often, and enclosing a photograph of their son Gordon. She also enclosed a copy of a letter from General Sandys saying that her son had been so gravely wounded when trying to save the horses when the wagon lines were being shelled that the shock had numbed the pain. He was smoking a cigarette when taken to the ambulance and made some joke about being trussed up like a fowl. The General said he could not go to see him personally as he was recovering from a wound himself, but that had her son lived he would certainly have been recommended for reward. It seems unfair that a man should be disqualified for an honour because he is killed, and rather hard on the parents.

The General also said that the subaltern, McKinsty, who was with her son was killed outright. I did not know him, he must have come as a replacement. The Soameses' grief made me realize that it is the parents who bear the burden in this war— not us.

I had a nice letter from the Colonel and from Parry. The Brigade seems to have changed altogether since I left, as they have had rather a rough time of it. Parry wrote,

> We are back again near the same old spot where your gluttony was your downfall (this means Arras). Your old battery has been most mutilated. After you deserted us you were followed by Chadwick (wounded), then Soames and McKinsty, finally Gifford took his section with him when the Battery amalgamated with B. C Battery, of course, is *'non est'* now. Of others you knew in the Brigade Taylour was hit in the arm. Wellesley and Menzies died of wounds as did poor old Weldon but Barnett hit at the same time seems to be getting on well. These, with Doc Wallis complete the tale of woe. By the way Taylour and McIvor emulated your example and got the M.C.

After lunching with the Soameses I went off to see the parents of one of our gunners at Millwall. The place was rather hard to find. I got out at West India Docks and walked about a couple of miles. The roads were crowded with men and women coming away from work, and it was getting dusk. I was struck by the courtesy of the dockers. Without exception everyone of whom I asked the way, dressed up as I was in my town suit, was most obliging and did his best to put me on the right way. I eventually found the people. A Zep bomb had fallen near and had broken their windows and brought down a good deal of the roof, which, of course, had upset them a good deal.

I went to see Harold at Hendon. He asked if I would like

him to take me up and show me all the tricks that an aeroplane could do. I said, 'Yes, if you let me wear your flying coat so that you will stop if I feel sick!' He started throwing the plane about, but when he did what he told me afterwards was the 'Immelmann Turn' I banged him on the shoulder which was the signal to stop. It nearly sent my stomach into my throat because at the top of an upward rush the plane suddenly did a sort of somersault and shot downwards. Apparently this enables an airman who is being chased to turn his plane round suddenly and attack his pursuer.

He took me round that afternoon to pay a duty call on Great Aunt Emily, the wife of Admiral Bowden-Smith, who evidently thought well of him for being in the Naval Air Service and chatted to him about his work. After a while she turned to me as a kindly afterthought and said, 'And where do you go to school?' I was a bit nonplussed not wishing to cause her embarrassment. Harold did the explaining and she, with the greatest composure, told me it was my fault for looking so absurdly young!

Yesterday I bumped into a school friend named Ball at Victoria Station. He is in the R.F.C. and has done great things. Such a nice fellow, quiet and unassuming. We used to do 'stinks' together. He had no less than three ribbons up and was just off to France. I had heard that he charges enemy planes head on and never swerves, on the theory that when the planes are about to collide the enemy always swerves upwards and he shoots it in the belly. [We heard later that he won the V.C. and from his last fight he never returned. It is possible that the German pilot worked on the same theory as he did.]

Last Wednesday was quite a remarkable day. First of all there was the lunch party at the Savoy Hotel given by Aunt Ethel to which a number of the family had been invited. A few days before, I had come across, in an old clothes shop, a woman's wig of hair of almost the same reddish colour as my own which I bought for 14s. This gave me the idea of dressing up for the party. So I went to a theatrical shop called Clarkson that morning and told them of my plan. They entered into the spirit of it and fitted me up as a young lady, only charging me ten bob. The man told me to walk boldly out and, to gain confidence, go to a policeman and ask the way. This I did. The Bobby was very polite and called me 'Miss' which put me quite at my ease. From there I went off to Liverpool Street station to meet Philip [a cousin] who had got leave from his regiment to come to the party. I had already wired to him that I would meet him there. When he got off the train and was looking round for me in the crowd I called his name from behind, in a gruff voice. He swung round but, not recognizing anyone, he looked mystified and moved on. I then came up behind him again and called his name in a female voice. He swung round again, and that was too much for me. I punched him in the ribs and doubled up with laughter until I saw the look of absolute horror on his face which made me realize that he took me for some mad woman. It was quite a job to make him realize who I was without letting the people around suspect anything. Finally, we went off and it was arranged that Philip was to explain to Aunt Ethel that I could not come to lunch but that he had brought along a lady friend in my place and hoped it would be all right.

We travelled by Underground. When we entered the carriage all the seats were taken. I was a little worried about holding a strap because my hands seemed rather too large, but fortunately a man jumped up and offered me his seat. We arrived at the prearranged meeting place where Philip introduced me to Aunt Ethel. I very nearly gave the game away because Jack, whom I thought was with his ship in the Mediterranean, was there. I was so pleased that I called out, 'Jack', but in the general hubbub no one heard. On crossing the road to the Savoy, Jack was near me, so I said that I was rather nervous of London streets. He gallantly took my arm and escorted me across safely. Lunch was a bit of an ordeal. Philip made some stupid remark which tickled me so much that the only thing was to bend my head so that my broad brimmed hat covered my face—with my shoulders shaking the others must have thought the poor girl had got hysterics as there was an embarrassed silence. Luckily it was soon over and the lunch ended without further incident. After changing at Clarksons I went to the station to see Aunt Ethel off and thank her for the lunch party. She was greatly surprised that I was the strange woman, but was very sporting over it all.

That evening dear Mrs Hadow had arranged a dinner party at her flat for five of us as her son Ken was home on short leave from his battery. She had booked a box at the theatre into which the five of us squashed and enjoyed a wonderful show called 'The Bing Boys' with George Robey. There was a remarkable interlude when four chaps calling themselves the Gresham Quartet strolled on with their hands in their pockets and sang two songs. The second was 'Drink to me only'. So beautifully did they sing that the encores from the whole theatre continued on and on for at least five minutes, but they never returned.

The period of sick leave was not yet to end; the second medical board was to insist on a further month's sick leave and told him that it was unlikely that he would be fit for active service again. This, in itself, was a depressing thought, but the situation was made worse by the low pay of a regular commission Second Lieutenant. So, a letter was sent by the author to the War Office asking them to cancel the regular commission and to allow him to retain his old seniority as a temporary First Lieutenant, thus getting a few shillings extra per day. The W.O. agreed.

The ensuing time was spent visiting friends and relations, including some in hospital. Among the latter was his cousin Oliver Leese, who had already been wounded once before, but was still in very good form: Leese was to become a general and to fight under Montgomery in the Second World War. He also visited Roberts from his battery: Roberts still had a splinter in his spine which needed periodic drainage.

The author also spent time in visiting the relatives of the men in his battery, and met once more Major Hawkshaw, who collected him from the station in his pony trap and entertained him in his west country home for some days; there Hawkshaw regaled him with many a queer tale of army life in Victorian days.

Another meeting, this time with General Princep, brought a promise from the General that he would ask for the author to be posted to the 65th Division, of which the General was C.R.A., in Ireland as soon he as was fit.

The next board, at his urgent request, passed the author fit for light duty, and on 22 January 1917 he was posted to one of Princep's brigades stationed at Kildare.

PART FOUR

Ireland

January to August 1917

CHAPTER 13

Bones and Dripping

I arrived at the R.A. Barracks Kildare last week and sampled
an Irish car to the Barracks. The Brigade Headquarters and two
batteries are here. The other batteries are stationed in Dublin
and Dundalk. As I have only been posted for light duty, the
Colonel put me on to looking after the messing of the men in
the four batteries, so I shall get some travelling about; he also
made me mess secretary to the officers' mess which I don't
relish. He is a curious chap, with a high-pitched voice and an
architect by profession. He is reported to have said when he
first arrived: 'I want all my officers to wear moustaches and
not look like a lot of smooth-faced flunkies.' I am afraid I can't
oblige him unless I wear a false one.

Less than half the officers have seen service overseas and the
batteries are in rather a primitive state. The Adjutant, Captain
Macknie, is a large red-faced fellow of about forty-five from the
Argentine where he was ranching—evidently with plenty of
money, judging by the jewels worn by his dusky, voluminous
wife. He and the Colonel have proper houses; the rest of us
have wooden huts with tin roofs—jolly cold just now with ice
and snow about. My batman is an excellent chap called Gill;
he reminds me of my first one, Locke. Like Locke, he was in
service as a footman to a family in Devonshire and knew Locke.
The yokels around are very friendly and I have had amusing
chats with several of them. One of the subalterns of the battery
to which I am attached is an old Oxford professor with bushy
eyebrows, bent shoulders and knows Cousin Harry. He is full

of dry humour and takes pride in being as unmilitary as possible. The other day he was reporting on one of his horses that had a wound on its near hindquarter. To the consternation of the Major, he said in a loud voice in front of the Battery, 'I have to report, sir, that one of my horses has a puncture in its left bottom.' He also caught out the Staff Captain when he inspected the cook-house where he (the professor) happened to be on duty. Seeing a lot of roast meat, the Staff Captain said, 'What do you do with the cracknels?' The Professor at once guessed that he knew nothing about cooking and asked politely, 'What exactly are cracknels, sir?' After a moment's hesitation he [Staff Captain] replied, 'I'm b . . . . . . d if I know,' at which the cooks and all joined in the laugh.

The messing job is quite interesting because of all the things one can do to improve the messing by stopping waste. Not a crumb must be thrown away. All the bones after the goodness has been boiled out of them are sent to certain firms who pay us for them, while every scrap of fat is collected and turned into dripping. Even the water that greasy plates are washed in is skimmed and the scum is put into the dripping tins. All of it is then sent to munition factories which pay well for it. In this way, with care, one can build up quite large funds for buying extra things to supplement the rations.

One of the pamphlets from the 'Bones and Dripping' Headquarters, stressing the importance of preventing waste, said that the Germans were so short of fats that they were rendering down the bodies of their dead soldiers to make nitro-glycerine, and it was hoped that it would not be necessary for us to do the same. Some of us were discussing this in the mess one evening and came to the conclusion that if we got killed we would be quite pleased if our bodies were used in this way in order to have another smack at the enemy.

A near catastrophe occurred last week. I discovered that the huge bin where we were storing our bones was empty— about £6 worth of bones had disappeared. We sent off a search party for the man who clears our dustbins and charged him with stealing the bones. In his broad Irish brogue, he said he thought the bones were put there for him to clear away. Old Macknie, looking very fierce, told him he was a liar and must return the bones. He said that would be impossible as all the dogs around would have taken them. He was then told to pay £6 for the ton of bones or be locked up. He then asked if we would accept half. We told him, 'No,' and would give him a week to get the money. He then asked if we would make it a fortnight. However, all was well because the cook who had gone to the station to see if the bones might be there had found them already in a truck bound for Dublin. How he was able to identify them I don't know, but he was quite certain they were ours. We had the documents rectified and were duly paid. We also thanked the dustman for having delivered them to the station for us!

On Friday I went to Marlborough Barracks in Dublin to inspect the messing of C Battery there. The Barracks are very fine and face on Phoenix Park. They are shared by the 12th Lancers and by a Squadron of King Edward's Horse. That night I dined at the mess. The officers of the 12th dine in mess kit, while the rest, of course, just have khaki. I happened to be sitting next to an old Major of the 12th. After a while he turned to me and said, 'I see you have been at the Front.' 'Yes, sir.' 'Very interesting. I suppose you went into trenches and things like that out there?' 'Yes, sir.' 'Very interesting, very interesting,' he said, gazing at me through his monocle. That was all, but kindly meant.

While in Dublin I had to walk through a rather slum area in search of the bone factory, and expected to be accosted by hostile Irishmen, but was unmolested. On return here, there were piles of new correspondence, including multifarious orders about messing which I distribute to the long-suffering batteries.

When on the train in Dublin I met General Princep who was interested to hear about my job. I told him about the missing bones episode which made him laugh. He asked if I would like to take over the messing job for all the artillery units of the Division which would mean visiting all the stations, such as Limerick, etc., where batteries were stationed. It would mean being stationed in Dublin so as to be in touch with the School of Cookery and the Headquarters. I told him I should like this very much if I could be attached to C Battery at Marlborough Barracks so that I could keep up with artillery work. He kindly said he would see what he could do about this.

The Adjutant called me in yesterday and after telling me that the officers' mess was the worst and most expensive he had ever experienced (he had some grounds for that, as I had left it all to the Mess Sergeant), he told me I was to be posted to C Battery. It is rather funny to think that having made a hash of running the officers' mess, I am to become Inspector of Messing to most of the Artillery in Ireland! Anyhow, I am delighted to go to C Battery whose C.O. is Major Lemmon, a first class soldier with a D.S.O.

I am now installed at Marlborough Barracks where every prospect pleases, and will have a chance of doing a little soldiering again and getting fit. The Major has readily agreed to my taking part in the Battery activities whenever I am free. The Captain is a bit of a character, named Hooghwinkel, who fought in Mexico before the war and has recently returned from the Dardanelles. The senior subaltern is a grand chap, an amusing hatchet-faced fellow named A. P. Cooper. He lost his left arm at the shoulder at Ypres, but managed to get out again in time for the Somme where he lost a bit of one foot. He is mad keen on horses and says we must go out hunting together. The other subaltern, MacDonald, a rather quiet sort of fellow, was at Glenalmond.

The King Edward's Horse officers are a jolly fine set. Many of them know Cousin Victor and admire him tremendously. One of them knew Harold when he was in the Cambridge Squadron.

I first met A.P. in the mess the evening I arrived. His empty sleeve was nattily pinned to the front of his coat. We talked and laughed together late into the night and went out riding next

12. *En route for the front. The train from Kantara to the railhead in Palestine.*

13.   *Some of the author's section in Palestine.*

14.   *The Wadi Nimrin, to the east of the Jordan bridgehead, where the temperature could reach 126° in the shade.*

day—he has a superb seat. When he first rode again after losing his arm he said he felt out of balance having to use his right. His sleeve was still empty so I ragged him about not wearing his wooden arm saying it was just swank. He said he did go out riding once with his arm on, first, bent at the elbow, but it kept banging him in the wind, so he straightened it downwards, then it kept banging his horse until it bolted. Since then he has never worn it.

Apparently, when he lost his arm, he was chatting to some-one with his hand in his pocket. The first thing he knew was seeing his arm suddenly swing backwards round his head.

There must be a great deal of poverty in Dublin. Whenever one goes out in the evenings, ragged little barefooted urchins timidly edge up and tap one's pockets whispering for pennies. One can't help feeling sorry for the little beggars, but after five or six such requests one's pockets are empty. It is possible their parents send them out to beg.

My new job starts tomorrow when I go to Fermoy to inspect three batteries there. There are batteries also at Kilkenny, and so on, all round the country. I attended an all-day cookery course all last week at Beggars Bush Barracks the other side of Dublin. There I met Major Bury Barry. He is I.Q.M.G.S., i.e. C. in C., Bones and Dripping. He took me to his home for lunch. Both he and his wife are charming people. The course was taken by a Captain Featherstone, formerly a quartermaster, a very jovial chap who rose from the ranks and has had forty-five years' service. It was most interesting. We learnt how to make puddings and things out of practically anything. Plum puddings were made from the sweepings of crumbs left on the tables which were first roasted in the oven. Of course, much else was added to make them tasty. I will have to send you some of the recipes.

I am in Limerick for a day or two having come from Fermoy. It has been great fun touring round. There are four batteries here. I arrived yesterday morning and inspected one battery in the afternoon, and have inspected two today. Tomorrow I hope to inspect the fourth and Brigade H.Q., and go to Clonmel on Monday.

It is St Patrick's Day with bands playing and crowds of men marching about. They seem quite peaceable and friendly all the same.

I left Limerick on Monday morning having spent a very pleasant time there. There were a cheery lot of officers there, and I met a Sergeant-Major who was in our Brigade in France. Just before the train pulled out of the station I heard much wailing and sobbing from a number of people seeing three men off, so I asked someone if they were emigrating to America or somewhere like that. He said, 'Oh! no. They are only going to Dublin for a visit.' Apparently this kind of send off is quite usual.

I had a ripping time in Clonmel. There was only one battery there. I arrived in the morning. The O.C., Captain Rodie, took me along later to the mess where there were five subalterns, and, after introducing me, said to them, 'We must do him proud otherwise he may report finding an old bone in one of our rubbish bins or something dreadful like that.' They insisted on my having lunch and dinner with them, and after dinner we had a concert. Captain Rodie, who, I learned afterwards, had been a professional entertainer, was at the piano and sang many music hall songs which we all joined in.

On my return here, I heard there was to be a meet of the Ward Union Stag Hounds next day about ten miles off. As an order had come out recently that officers were not allowed to hunt their own chargers, A.P. and I went off to hire two horses. We arrived at the meet at 1.30. It was a lovely day and a turn-out of about 100. The first run was very short, so we had a second which was a splendid one. Practically all the obstacles were ditches.

On Friday I went to Dundalk to inspect the D.A.C. messing. They showed me about five tons of potatoes in a cellar which were all starting to sprout and asked what they should do about them. I really did not know, but said they should be planted at once. The only ground they had were the parade ground and some tennis lawns so I gave instructions for the tennis lawns to be dug up and the potatoes planted there. I hope they get a good crop! After that, I inspected the Battery and returned to the hotel to write up the reports and also started getting my messing notes ready for printing.

What rotten luck about Philip having his leg blown off and dying in a prison hospital. It must have been awful. Poor Aunt Kathleen.

I had a most enjoyable week since last writing. Monday was spent inspecting C Battery's messing and getting my booklet on messing ready. On Tuesday I went to Kildare and, after inspecting one battery there, went on to Divisional Artillery H.Q. at the Curragh where I had lunch. The Staff Captain (under whom I work) is a perfect brick. He told me I was absolutely my own master and could go to any place I wanted where there are batteries and stay as long as I thought fit. He suggested that my visits might coincide with race meetings, etc. I gave him my booklet on messing which is to be entitled 'Army Messing and How It Should Be Carried Out'. He thought a high sounding title like that would help to carry weight. I suggested adding at the bottom 'By One Who Knows', but he thought that would be asking too much! He is going to have it printed. He also said he would arrange to send me to London to have my bullet out if the Medical Board advised its extraction, so I returned here with a light heart and went hunting next day.

CHAPTER 14

Fun and Games

Please excuse my bad writing, but I stupidly broke my right collar bone yesterday, so my arm is strapped to my side and I can only move my hand from the wrist.

The other day I had a letter from Uncle Julian who gave me a lot of introductions to people in Ireland, but the only one in Dublin was a Sir George Brooke, so I went round there to tea. He is an old man of nearly sixty with a son of about thirty and two daughters in their early twenties. They were very friendly and told me to call again whenever I was free. Old Sir George suggested that I should call on General Hutchinson who had been in the 11th with Uncle Julian and was now Chief of Staff to the C. in C. Mahon, and who lived in the Under Secretary's house quite close to our barracks. (It was his office that had sent out the order stopping officers hunting their chargers.) So I called next day about tea-time. He came to the door himself and, when I introduced myself, he looked at me rather oddly for a moment or two, which made me feel that I should not have barged in like this; he then invited me in and introduced me to his wife, who put me quite at ease. He soon thawed and it was seven before I realized it was getting late. The wonderful thing was that he asked me if I was going out with the Ward Union on Saturday. I said, 'No, sir!' He said, 'Why not?' I replied, 'Because of the order that officers may not hunt their chargers, and I can't afford to hire horses any more.' To which he said, 'But surely you could be doing reconnaissance in that part of the country?' That has solved our problem, and I told

A.P. at once on my return, which cheered him enormously.

The Hutchinsons invited me to dinner the next day, and took me to a play at the Gaiety Theatre, an amateur show in aid of the Red Cross. There was a Lady Conyngham in our party, a dear old soul, who warned me about lending money to one of the 12th Lancer officers at our barracks who was well known in the racing circles. I thanked her, although, of course, I have no money to lend. We occupied a box at the theatre. There were a lot of K-nuts at the show including Mahon, the C. in C. He was in a box with Lady Londonderry and others and was looking very glum. The story went that he had been persuaded by Lady L. to address a temperance meeting that afternoon and afterwards to sign the pledge!

Well yesterday was the most glorious day's hunting that any-one could wish for. Now that we had the all clear about horses, A.P. took me round the stables on the Friday evening and said I could take any horse I fancied. I spotted a great chestnut mare that was a lead horse of one of the gun teams. It stood nearly seventeen hands. A.P. said, 'Now my lad, I will let you take her out if you promise not to over-ride her. She is not in training for hunting.' He had his own charger. We insured them both and off we went next morning with two other subalterns on their own chargers, on our 'reconnaissance'. I felt remarkably highly perched like a pea on a giraffe.

There was a tremendous turn-out at this meet— about 150— including the Lord Lieutenant, Lord Wimborne. To my surprise several people came up exclaiming 'Oh! Yorkshire Lass. Where has she been lately?' This was my chestnut mount —evidently a well-known hunter. They seemed rather shocked when I told them that she was now a puller of guns.

What a mighty day it was! A fifteen mile point without a check. Yorkshire Lass went like a stag. Forgotten was A.P.'s admonition with this great hunter whisking me over banks and ditches, eating up field after field. Then I saw in front of me a rider and horse disappear when trying to fly a fifteen foot ditch. 'Come on, Yorkshire Lass, we'll show them.' Over ditch, horse and rider we went, but the pace had been too great. She just failed to clear the further bank and came down on her nose while I shot through the air landing on the back of my head the far side. Somewhat dazed I saw Yorkshire Lass standing over me and felt a pain in my shoulder as I started to mount. My attention was turned to the fellow emerging from the ditch swearing at me for jumping over him and I vaguely remember returning him a few choice expressions of derision before setting off again. I realized my collar bone had gone, but as it was my right one it did not bother me. The mare would have cleared that jump all right had she been in training. After another six fields or so I dismounted and led her, as she was quite beat. They caught the stag only half a mile further on so we missed by only half a mile.

One of the hunt very kindly came back with me, because I was evidently raving a bit owing to the bang on my head, and we stopped at the house of one of his friends where we had some refreshments after which I was able to walk my mare home (about six miles).

Poor Yorkshire Lass lay down for a week after that great day with the Ward. A.P. did not half berate me for such behaviour. She is, however, quite fit again now and A.P. may, perhaps, let me take her out again.

The Doctor told me to take ten days' sick leave owing to the effects of the concussion. My brain seemed to work rather spasmodically and I got headaches. Unfortunately a new order has just come in saying that no sick leave may be given under any circumstances whatsoever. Anyone unfit must go to hospital and then straight back to duty. The Staff Captain noticed that I was off colour when I saw him last Wednesday and told me to take a rest. The trouble is my Medical Board is due to sit in a day or two and may refuse to pass me fit to go abroad.

On Easter Monday A.P. and I went to Fairyhouse races. We could not get a vehicle to take us so took a tram into Dublin. There we sighted a jaunting car and got in. As we approached the G.P.O. in Sackville Street, which had been burned in the

Rebellion and was only a shell, we saw a crowd gazing at a queer-coloured flag on top. I thought it must be a suffragette flag and wondered why there was all this excitement, so asked some of the crowd, who told us it was the Sinn Fein flag and they were celebrating the anniversary of the Rebellion! Fortunately, they took my *faux pas* in great good humour, and we got some friendly waves from them as we passed on to the races where we had an enjoyable afternoon.

My collar bone is not hurrying itself to heal up. The Medical Board which I attended three days ago would not give their verdict, but said that I would have to wait another month, in any case, because of my collar bone, which seemed absurd. I told them that if I were posted out East it would get better on the ship.

I am sending you a copy of my booklet on messing. It is in execrable grammar and in military jargon only to be excelled by the F.A.T. [Field Artillery Training]! Anyhow, the standard of messing is improving in spite of it.

As you see, I am in Limerick on my rounds again. I have been getting such friendly welcomes, and am always invited to join them at their messes. Last night four of us went to a local performance in the town which was quite an uproarious affair.

When down at Limerick, I met Captain Neligan of the R.I.C., who was staying at the same hotel. He had brought a troop of police down to stop some rows that were going on there. He had been shot through the lung in the Dublin Rebellion and consequently is not very friendly with the Sinn Feiners. His headquarters are the R.I.C. Barracks in Dublin, which are quite close to ours, and he asked me to dine with him at their mess next week. After inspecting two units in Limerick, I had a wire from A.P. telling me to join him at the Punchestown races the following day, so I caught the first train to Dublin in the morning. About twelve miles from Dublin, I noticed a crowd at a station, so got out to find there was a branch line and the last special was leaving for Punchestown in two minutes. I just had time to collect my bag and catch the last carriage as the train moved off. We arrived at the grandstand a quarter of an hour before the start of the first race and there I met A.P. The crowds were tremendous and among them many whom I knew. I have never seen such a conglomeration of female beauty. What with the lovely horses and the glorious sunshine, it was like a sort of fairyland. The course is one of the stiffest in the world.

On Friday A.P. and I went to the theatre. When leaving late that night, a whole crowd of youngsters came marching along the road with banners, 'Up the Rebels' and 'Hoch! the Kaiser', and seemed very pleased with themselves. Two subalterns who were walking behind us on the pavement seemed to have imbibed too freely. The marchers spotted us and as they passed, one of them clipped one of the two behind on the chin shouting, 'Up the Rebels'. We stopped these two just in time from rushing bald-headed at the crowd, otherwise things might have become unpleasant. Anyhow all passed off quite amicably.

I have had a bit of luck. A wire arrived for me on the 4th [May] ordering me to report at the War Office for an interview with the Inspector of Army Catering at 11 a.m. on the 5th in connection with the appointment of army caterers in France. Three hours before the boat left, the Staff Captain phoned me to tell me to take a week's unofficial leave, so not only did I get leave but a free ticket to London. The telegram caused much amusement in the mess and I was advised to stuff a pillow in front of my stomach and put on some wax moustaches.

The boat left at 10 p.m. and we had on board the crews of two German submarines who had been captured a few hours before. There had been three submarines, but one escaped.

On arrival at the War Office, I found about twelve others to be interviewed, mostly old quartermasters, etc. Apparently there were four vacancies to be filled, and all home Divisions had been asked to send in names. My name had been sent in by the 65th Division. All the others seemed on pins and needles about it. Evidently the pay is good, with blue tabs, etc. As I had no wish for such a job I was able to survey the others with some amusement. When my turn came and I was ushered in, the Major looked rather startled, and said, 'Did you write this?' pointing to the booklet on messing he had on his desk. When I acknowledged authorship, he cleared his throat and after a few ums and ahs, said that I had been sent for about a job of army catering in France. I replied that perhaps the job would be more suitable for a hotel-keeper or quartermaster, with which sentiment he whole-heartedly agreed.

So here I am in Godalming. The weather is glorious. Mollie was in bed all Sunday. Dorothy and I walked over to tea with the Fairtloughs. Lance was there, minus his foot. He told me that Cousin Howard [his father] was killed leading his Territorial Battalion in an attack on the Bosch lines. It seems silly to have let an old chap like him go to France. There he was limping along with the aid of a stick in front of his men, just a sitting duck. Lance hopes to have a new foot put on in a month or two.

That reminds me. A.P. went into hospital on Monday to have a slice more of his arm removed. There is not much left of it— only about one inch from the shoulder. He ought to be on the mend when I get back. The Brooke daughters said they would go to see him and take him flowers.

Before coming down here I had lunch with the Soameses. Mr Soames had to leave immediately afterwards for a secret session of Parliament. Then on to the Club, when who should slap me on the back but Major Walker, who commanded C Battery in the 48th Brigade. We (i.e. A Battery) always worked with C. At Arras he left for a horse battery and I met him again on the Somme the day before I was hit. He gave me a lot of news about everyone, including Major Erskine, who was wounded and is doing a job in Town.

On my arrival in Dublin, after a visit to Limerick on 22

May, I found that A.P. had not returned from London, where he had gone to get a new arm fitted, but had entered me for the Grand Jumping Competition, Ballsbridge. Unfortunately Yorkshire Lass had gone lame while I was away and was not fit for the show. As A.P. had not returned, Captain Hooghwinkel, who has jumped at the New York Horse Show, decided to ride his grey.

A.P. returned on Saturday morning and determined to jump that afternoon. I could not get over till later because Romanes was taking me sailing with four youngsters from a Boy Scout Club which he is interested in.

I got to the Bazaar at seven where I met A.P. and we went on the aerial rope. A man is supposed to hang on with both hands—one on each of the handles which are attached to a wheel balanced on a wire and whizz down it starting about thirty feet above the ground and landing on a mattress some fifty yards away. Cooper, having only one arm, could only hold one handle, so, to make up, I held the other. Owing to my wanky collar bone I had to hold on with my left hand. The people operating it at first refused us and then agreed, but shouted to the crowd that they would not be responsible for results. Off we went, but on the way I found I could not hold on any longer with my left hand so had to swing my right up, too, and then thought A.P. might be slipping so gripped him with my legs to give him some support. We arrived safely with a rush. A.P. was very thankful for the extra support. The people seemed quite excited about it and said their hearts were in their mouths! A number of them insisted on taking us to a party afterwards. We were the only ones in uniform. It was a very jolly affair, but what amused us were three young Irishmen whom we were chatting with who told us that they had been in the rebellion and had only recently come out of prison! All most friendly.

CHAPTER 15

A Rumpus or Two

I started proper work with the Battery on 5 June and went out on drill order. The Major has given me the job of training the twenty-four best layers in the Battery. My collar bone was X-rayed last Tuesday and I have to go to the Military hospital for massage each day. This will probably last a fortnight, then it should be all right.

My application to go abroad again, after being held up for a fortnight at Brigade Headquarters, was returned, saying it had to be rendered in quadruplicate, so I wrote it out three times more. The original copy had been signed by the Major and since he had gone to London for a week, Captain Hooghwinkel signed the other three as he was acting O.C. The whole lot were returned yet again, saying the application could not be considered because of the different signatures! Other officers who have applied to go to the front have received similar obstruction.

Raymond Brooke, the son of the old man, rang me up the other day to ask if I would take a small part in a play for charity being put on at Glenmaroon, the home of the Ernest Guinesses, just across the Park. I said I would be delighted, so he asked me to lunch at his club in Kildare Street which seemed crammed full of old fossils and crusty old men and Generals of about eighty, just like Madame Tussaud's. He gave me my part which only consists of three lines—as a grocer's boy at the Pit door of a theatre. I have stuck one of the notices of the Play up in the mess and written my name down in large letters as one of the chief actors, with a note at the bottom that all officers are expected to attend! I think most of them will come.

A.P. had his operation last Tuesday, but on Friday, when I thought he might be well enough to have visitors, he appeared at the Barracks. He has had a nerve removed and is to have the stitches out in a few days. Meanwhile he gads about. His horse has arrived from England and he is going to jump it at the next Competition. I shall enter Yorkshire Lass and Hooghwinkel is going to enter his grey, so the Battery will be well represented.

Yesterday afternoon, being Saturday, A.P. suggested that we should go for a gallop across the Park. I told him I couldn't as I was orderly officer. On his pointing out that the Major was away and nothing ever happened on Saturday afternoon, I finally agreed to go. On our return, at about 5 p.m., the Sergeant-Major came rushing up in some agitation saying that orders had just come about trouble to be expected on Sunday morning and that all troops were to stand to. He said the Major had returned and had been looking for me. I asked whether the Major had made any dispositions. He said 'No.' With a gasp of relief, I ordered all the guns out and, with A.P.'s help, trained them on different parts of the perimeter walls which seemed most vulnerable and then dashed over to the Major and reported the action taken. He seemed very satisfied, and said that, as a matter of fact, he had been wondering where I was! That was a near thing; I said to A.P. afterwards: 'So much for your assurances about Saturday afternoons.' The King Edward's Horse provided the guards who were dished out with canvas bandoliers containing a hundred rounds in addition to their ordinary bandolier equipment.

Nothing happened at the Barracks. We saw a few heads pop over the walls, but they probably saw the muzzles of our guns glaring at them and reported back accordingly.

There was a row this morning at Beresford Place, but it was dealt with by the R.I.C.; one Inspector was killed—struck on the head from behind. A rotten business.

I have just had a very pleasant two days in London on a free ticket. A message came from the War Office to attend an investiture at Buckingham Palace, so off I went catching the night boat and presented myself at B.P. on Tuesday morning. There must have been over fifty of us; among them was Captain Ling, now a Major. We had had instructions to take white gloves. We were taken up a great flight of stairs into a large long anteroom, where we were told to put on the left glove and carry the other and after presentation to walk backwards five paces before marching off. We moved along in a queue and then waited for our names to be called. The King looked very tired. It must be pretty difficult to think of something to say to each one of us. I did not catch what he said to me when he put on the medal, so just replied 'Yes, sir.' (I thought afterwards that this might have been inappropriate if, for instance, he had said, 'Jolly good show,' or something like that.) I nearly forgot about shaking hands, but fortunately just spotted his hand coming forward.

The acting has been great fun. Glenmaroon is a beautiful house, and their private theatre is a very fine one.

The pukkha show was held last night to a packed house. Quite a bunch from Marlborough Barracks were there, including Colonel Dick of the K.E.H. and our Major and his wife. There were several generals and other staff officers. I had to chew an orange on the stage and found I could shoot the pips at the audience by pressing them between my finger and thumb. This wasn't in the script, but it helped to liven the show, especially when a pip bounced off the bald head of a staff colonel.

I had been over to lunch with the Guinesses on several occasions. They have two very pretty daughters in their early teens. During an afternoon stroll I happened to tell Ernest Guiness that I was going into military hospital to have my bullet extracted. (It has been giving me a bit of trouble lately, a sort of dull pain, which causes a feeling of exhaustion and tends to make me flop: nothing serious, but it will be as well to get rid of it.) The chap at the hospital had said after an X-ray that it would be an easy job as the bullet was only two and a half inches inside, near the spine. Mr Guiness urged me strongly not to go near that hospital, but to go to his surgeon, Colonel Wheeler, who runs a private hospital for officers in Dublin and is reckoned to be one of the finest surgeons in Ireland or Britain. He said he would arrange for me to see him.

Last week a great lanky Australian subaltern in the King Edward's Horse greeted me. 'We are going to chuck you in the Liffey.' On asking him what for, he said, 'You, with your wide mouthed chatter to the Colonel the other night about how all the officers at Kildare had to turn out for physical jerks before breakfast; he has ordered us all to do lance drill each morning before breakfast.' I told him that my bedroom overlooked the parade ground and I would gladly give them a smile of encouragement from my window. And there they were next morning doing their drill. They have been jolly decent about it and I have not yet sampled the waters of the Liffey—except in the form of stout.

I have just returned from a trip to Kilworth and Limerick with Dunn, who is taking over the messing job from me, and found a letter waiting for me telling me to ring up Colonel Wheeler as soon as possible. He said he would try to see me on Saturday at one, so down I went. He is a very kindly fellow and kept ringing up all sorts of people to try to arrange for me to enter his hospital as soon as possible. It was finally arranged through the O.C. Expeditionary Forces K.G.V. Hospital that I should report at Colonel Wheeler's hospital in Upper FitzWilliam Street tomorrow, so I am packing my traps.

The battery is leaving Dublin on Tuesday for the Curragh for three weeks' Brigade training, and then a week's practice camp. I am not sorry about missing it, although I should love the camping, etc., but we should be in the clutches of that ghastly Colonel who seems to have a special dislike of anyone who has seen active service. The K.E.H. have promised to take care of my kit at the Barracks.

I came into hospital last Monday. Colonel Wheeler has

decided not to operate. He took great pains to locate the bullet by a stereoscopic method and found it was over four inches in. This would mean digging into the lung and even then he would not guarantee being able to extract it without messing me up unduly. He asked me how about three weeks' leave instead. I said this would suit me down to the ground. Although such leave has been abolished, it is probable that his recommendation will not be contested.

I remember telling Captain Hooghwinkel, when orders came for the Battery to proceed to the Curragh for Brigade training, that I had no intention of going; his reply was that I had jolly well got to obey or be court martialled. I had heard a funny story about Hooghwinkel. On being introduced to the Colonel on first arrival, the Colonel said to him, 'I am very interested in Church work.' So Hooghwinkel, who had heard that the Colonel was supposed to have been an architect, said, 'Oh really, sir, have you built many?' The Colonel corrected him sharply saying he was referring to church services, to which Hooghwinkel replied piously, 'Oh, and so am I, and so am I." The old rascal!

I am half way through my leave. The Medical Board in Ireland, on the advice of Colonel Wheeler, gave me this sick leave and advised an early transfer to a tropical climate. They told me, however, that I have to return to Ireland for light duty until October or November. Before leaving, I called on the Guinesses to thank them as it was through their help that I went to Colonel Wheeler's hospital; then had dinner with the Bury Barrys at the club.

On arrival in Town, I went to the War Office as my chief concern on this leave was to make certain of getting out East as soon as possible. Otherwise it might mean permanent home service in Ireland .On arrival at the W.O., I decided to aim high, and did not care if I got in a row or not. I asked for an interview with General Hutchinson, who is now M.G. i/c Administration. He was just hanging his coat when I was ushered in. He was as nice as he always is and asked what he could do for me. I told him that I had applied three times to get abroad again without result and wanted to get out as soon as possible. He rang up Colonel Younge, who is Adjutant-General, and asked him to do what he could for me. I went straight to Colonel Younge who asked me who I was. When I told him, he said he was at Bradfield with you and asked how you were.

When I told him of the failure of my application to go abroad, he looked very hard at me. I knew it was a bit risky saying this because one colonel in Ireland had already been court martialled for not allowing his officers to go out again. Anyhow it will be a good thing if an inquiry is made into our Brigade because our Colonel would not come too well out of it. After looking at my papers, he said, 'Humph! You have just come out of hospital and the Medical Board has ordered you three weeks' sick leave and then two months' light duty, and yet you ask to be sent abroad.' After glaring at me again, he merely said, 'You will go to Egypt.' With a light heart, I rushed to Euston for my bags and just got to Waterloo, where Aunt Ethel was waiting for me to catch the train for Godalming; there I spent a blissful week-end.

On returning to Town, I went to see Arthur Hamilton who had been burnt while serving in the Tanks. He is in a swagger nursing home in Park Lane and was lying on a couch on the lawn where I tried to give him his tea, but most of it spilled down his neck because he would keep chuckling at my attempts. I envied him his beautiful V.A.D.s, but was only allowed to stay half an hour.

Yesterday I had the most delightful surprise *rencontre*. Who should it be but Sergeant Sheward, who had been wounded two days after me—had his left forearm blown off. He is out of the Army—a well-dressed, fine, soldierly-looking man. He, Sergeant Bliss and Hobbs all joined my section together. Three Londoners and what a grand trio they were. We went to see *Theodore and Co.* at the Gaiety, which we both enjoyed immensely and then had some supper. Sheward and I had so much to talk about. Our Brigade had been specially mentioned and was

15. *The Amman Raid. Horsemen of the Army of the King of the Hedjaz at Es Salt. (Imperial War Museum).*

16. *Inspection by General Falkenheim, the commander of the Turko-German forces in 1917. The sentry does not appear to like him.*

17. *The author, with captured Ger-man medals, outside General Liman von Sanders' quarters after the Germans fled.*

18. *German GHQ Staff in 1918. Standing on the bottom step are: Liman von Sanders, C-in-C; Major von Papen; Talaat Pasha, former leader of the Young Turks.*

chosen, after the Somme, to train officers and N.C.O.s (a great honour). Several of the old lot had been killed, mostly, as usual, the best ones. He told me that Bliss had got a commission. Hobbs is still a gunner. None of them got a decoration. Personally, I thought Bliss deserved one more than anyone in the Battery. He was always so calm when fellows got hit under heavy shell fire, always doing the right thing, and was the means of saving several lives. Incidentally, he saved Sheward's life by tying a bootlace round the stump of his arm and twisting it tight. He was the one with me when Nodder and the Battery Clerk were killed on the Somme.

Sergeant Sheward told me that they heard at the Battery at first that I had been killed but when they heard I was wounded they waited up all night, like the dear chaps they were, looking at each stretcher as it passed by to see if they could see me and give me a cheery word or two. But I was taken round another way, so missed that pleasure.

On getting back to Marlborough Barracks on the 9th, I found A.P. and Romanes looking well, and got such a welcome from everyone. They all seemed to know I was off to Egypt shortly. A.P. told me that several others in the Brigade had slammed in their applications to get out again, and that Davies from D Battery at Kildare, a very nice chap, who had had a row with the Colonel, had already managed to get away and was now in London on embarkation leave for Egypt, so we may be on the same draft. Although I am under orders for Egypt, I was frightened lest the M.B. would not pass me fit so phoned up Colonel Wheeler, who gave me a certificate of fitness for Egypt.

In Dublin yesterday I ran into a school friend who broke the [school] long jump record before war broke out. He is in the Infantry and has no right to be alive, because, when they were charging an enemy trench, he got fifteen bullets in his stomach from a machine gun at about ten yards. Eight went through him and seven stayed inside. After lying there in the mud for some time he was hit on the head with a shell fragment which cracked his skull. He was dragged into his own lines that night and was unconscious for eleven weeks, during which time his stomach was able to heal up. Now he is trying to persuade the Medical Board to pass him fit to go out again.

A.P. and I had what will probably be our last ride together this afternoon, unless he gets out to Egypt, too. We went through some lovely woods with deep valleys and steep hills—very invigorating.

A.P. had a lurid story to tell of the so-called Brigade training. Apparently the Batteries had to march south from the Curragh by independent routes. Hooghwinkel was in command of the Battery. When passing through a town they were most hospitably received by the townsfolk, who gave them a slap up lunch with beer all round. After lunch they moved off. It was a hot sunny day and naturally, after such a good lunch, the men were hot and a bit red in the face, when round a bend they found the Colonel sitting on his horse waiting for them. He said the Sergeant-Major was drunk, told Hooghwinkel to put him under arrest, and then disappeared. On the following day, as the Sergeant-Major was a very fine soldier and everything ran smoothly when he was about, Hooghwinkel reinstated him. Sure enough around another bend, there was the Colonel waiting, and saw the Sergeant-Major riding in his accustomed place. The Colonel was livid and asked A.P. if he was prepared to take command of the Battery (over Hooghwinkel's head). A.P. replied, 'Yes, sir, if you give me a specific command in writing to do so.' That gave the Colonel a bit of a shock. He then ordered the whole Battery to dismount, tether their horses, and form up in a field. Whereupon he started to slang them as the worst Battery he had ever come across, and finally said, 'I don't blame you men. When I look at your officers I am sorry for you'. A.P. said he felt so blazing mad that he started forward towards the Colonel, but one of his sergeants caught him by the coat saying, 'Steady, sir'. Finally, the Colonel turned to one of the sergeants and said, 'Dismiss the Battery'. After dismissal there was a dead silence and then one of the men shouted out, 'Three Hoots for the Colonel'. The Colonel turned as white as a sheet and left in a hurry.

Hooghwinkel was court martialled. The Court sat at Cork. Apparently no one at the mess would speak to the Colonel. When the Court asked Hooghwinkel about his war service, he told them of his Mexican and Dardanelles campaigns. The Court then asked the Colonel about his and he had to admit he had none.

As Hooghwinkel was technically in the wrong for reinstating the Sergeant-Major, he was found guilty, but the sentence was, 'Loss of one day's seniority!'

Among the papers are two letters from A. P. Cooper. The first, from Ireland, was written a few months later from Moore Park near Fermoy. One reads as follows:

What fun we had on Quinn's old 'quods' with the Ward. Since Christmas I have had, on an average, two days with hounds every week. One day with the Duhallow, when I was mounted on a magnificent mare, I was given the pate which now hangs in my hut. I was also offered a mount in the Duhallow Point to Point. We started in a hell of a gale and at the hell of a pace over banks as big as Shebeens. At the third, a fellow crossed me and I came a cropper on the far side. While lying there with the rest of the field coming over I heard 'Och! the poor fellow, just fancy forty horses changing feet on the pit of his stomach.' 'Oh! begorroh, and he desthroyed entoirely.' 'Devil a bit, these Cassidies have got constitutions of iron'.

One day was very hot and the hounds couldn't own the line at all. Another cover was tried, but never a note from any of them. The situation was pithily summed up by an old pub-owning farmer who said 'There's no blody stink for the dogs today'.

I love these South Irish people and am enjoying life to the

full. Nevertheless, I do hope I shall get out soon. True, about a month ago I was on the verge of committing moral suicide —marriage. Today, I am further off than I have been for years. You, of course, my boy, have a long time to wait and much experience to gain before you may consider the awful proposition. Bad cess to it!

The next letter was from somewhere in France.

What with the Colonel and O.C., B.A.C. to which I was lately attached, I found life unbearable in Ireland and at last managed to get out here. I have just returned from a ride through poor old Bailleul. It makes one sick to see a place, where one has enjoyed so well the lighter side of war, in such a pitiable state. Flat, flat as a pancake, and all around reminds me of my first view of Fricourt.

There was also a note that A. P. Cooper was involved in a gas attack and, after apparent recovery, he later lost his sight and died soon afterwards. So passed a gay and gallant friend.

PART FIVE

Egypt and Palestine
September 1917 to June 1918

CHAPTER 16

Alexandria

We landed here [Alexandria] on 6 September, and I had to come into the General Hospital for a small operation through my nose because of an abscess inside my cheek bone, contracted at Taranto. It is a nuisance because I shall probably miss seeing some of my travelling companions before they leave.

It was a most delightful trip right through France and Italy. The train journey from Cherbourg to Taranto in the heel of Italy took ten days, including two days at rest camps.

We had a roughish passage from Southampton in a rather small ship. On arrival next morning in Cherbourg, we marched some four miles to the camp. The drafts were under their own officers and the rest of us consisting mostly of doctors, padres, gunners and a few cavalrymen, marched up together in fours at the rear of the column. After that we were free to do more or less as we liked and were treated most considerately. We entrained next day.

Davies and I shared a compartment with an amusing fellow called Stewart from the Glasgow Yeomanry. In the next compartment were Captain Driscoll, R.F.A., Captain Brooks, R.F.A. (who had travelled in many parts of the world, including Tibet), and a huge wild Irishman named Ashby, R.A.M.C., who besides being a surgeon was a rugby international. The six of us became friends and did most things together. Ashby, with his riproarious songs and general high spirits, was a great asset. We travelled at a leisurely pace through some beautiful country, stopping every so often for refreshments and to stretch our legs. Everyone from the French villages through which we passed, from two years old to eighty, turned out to wave to us. At some places, they gave the men wine. Many of the men sat on the footboards, and a few sportsmen climbed on to the roofs of the carriages. We passed several Bosch prisoners who waved to us in a most friendly manner. At one station I went to a French Red Cross place to get some ointment for an inflamed eye and was tended by a beautiful countess who was working there. The train was very slow and no one thought of getting in until some time after it started. We stopped for twenty-four hours at a rest camp at St Germaine. It was very hot, so many of us trooped down to a picturesque river where we had a glorious bathe and basked in the sun afterwards.

There was a large crowd at Lyons Station to greet us as we were almost the first lot of British troops to travel this way. While the train was waiting in the station there was much badinage between the troops and the populace. Many invitations were shouted to ladies in the crowd to board the train. None of us were supposed to leave the train, but one of the doctors, quite a small chap, jumped out, rushed to the crowd, threw a large lady over his shoulder and started running back with her to the train, amidst cheers from us and the crowd. As he ran, he tripped over a railway line, falling flat with the girl on top of him, causing great merriment from everyone, including the girl.

When we stopped in a small station at Amberieux in the afternoon quite a number of French girls came to greet us. Two rather nice sisters, the Mlles. Gonnet, came and chatted to Driscoll and me. I took a photo of them and they gave us their address so that I could send them the snaps.

When we reached Modane in Italy, we were greeted with frantic waves from the Italian youth and beauty. The train had stopped and they were on the other side of the fence. They kept calling us to come over to them like the sirens to the Argonauts. Since we were bound to the train by the strictest orders, and I did not wish them to think we spurned their friendly advances, I shouted in desperation, *'Non permitioso'*, in the hope that they would understand. Anyhow, most of us were leaning half out of the windows and waving our appreciation of their welcome.

We stopped another twenty-four hours at the rest camp at Faenza. Stewart and I decided to spend the night in the hotel. It was a curious mosquelike place, but quite comfortable. We were very surprised on leaving after breakfast to find that our bill came to the equivalent of only 2s. 6d. each!

On the way southwards. Stewart and I thought we would like to ride on the engine. The engine-driver beckoned us on board, and we had a very pleasant ride for the next hour or two. He opened a bottle of chianti and invited us to have a swig. We both thought it tasted exactly like vinegar.

On arrival at Taranto the six of us managed to occupy two tents next to each other and were able to mess together. The transit [hospital] camp was very overcrowded and the sanitation and food were both pretty bad. The doctors proposed to write a strong letter to the Camp Commandant who was a colonel and a bigwig, but they finally funked signing it except for Ashby who, although only a subaltern, signed it alone. I happened to be in the camp office when Ashby was called in. I heard their conversation.

'Are you the author of this letter?'

'Yes, sorr.'

'What the hell do you mean by it?'

'If you come round the camp with me, I will show you, sorr.'

He was the means of improving matters quite considerably.

We were there for five days, and the bathing was glorious. It was so warm we could stay in for two hours or more. There was a large number of V.A.D.s at the hospital camp—mostly passing through. We were not allowed to speak to them except in the water, which suited us because the officers' beach and theirs were next to each other. While swimming about, who should I see but Miss Geoffries, the V.A.D. who nursed me at Oxford. She was going to Salonika. It was her second attempt, as her ship had been torpedoed the first time. She was picked up after two hours: she cannot swim a stroke but her cork belt kept her up. She seemed to take the whole affair very lightly, although she lost all her kit. Driscoll also knew one of the nurses who introduced us to a friend. On the last day Driscoll, Stewart and I, with these three, got leave to go to the town about four miles off. We had tea there, at the Italian Naval Officers' Club, and, after some shopping, returned about seven in a motor launch. The next day we embarked and the V.A.D.s went to their ship. As both ships were there all day, and barely half a mile apart, with no boat available in which to go over and say goodbye, I was deputed to carry dispatches, so put them in a cigarette tin, tied it on the top of my head with my tie and swam over breast stroke, so as not to wet the tin. It took me nearly half an hour. On approaching the other ship, I saw crowds of faces by the ship's rails watching this queer object approaching, and an orderly came down the gangway, to whom I handed the letters. By luck, a launch was leaving for shore that very minute, and dropped me quite close to our ship.

The sea voyage was dull with no alarms. I was put in charge of a boat, but another officer asked if he could take it over as most of the men were of his draft. To this I readily agreed, since it would be more fun as a freelance if we were torpedoed. As, however, General Salmond of the R.F.C. had been allocated to my boat, I thought it would be courteous to tell him about my handing it over. He asked me why, and I told him the reason. I think he must have told the O.C. Troops, because I received orders to take charge of the starboard foredeck with thirteen rafts and fifteen men to each. We had to impress on the men not to chuck the rafts over too soon and also to fix their cork belts as high as possible under the armpits. Going round my lot I saw a chap with his belt fixed round the lower part of his stomach so I bellowed at him through my megaphone, 'Do you really want to float bottom upwards?' The resulting guffaws assured me that they would not need reminding again.

There were about two dozen nurses in our ship. Although

there was dancing to a gramophone in the evening, I did not feel like joining in as I have an abscess in my head which was playing up. One of the doctors gave me some bromide to help me get some sleep. Since the night was hot, most of us slept on deck. The nurses were allocated a raised hatch in the middle of the deck while we men lay all around it. For the nurses, it must have felt like being on a raft surrounded by a school of porpoises—or sharks, perhaps!

Ashby and Stewart were unfortunately kept back at Taranto, but should be coming along on the next ship.

Most of my journey companions left after about ten days here [Alexandria] as they were passed fit for general service, while I was put on the T.B. [temporary base] list. However, there may be a chance of being passed fit at the next Medical Board. Unfortunately, I have just heard that I am to be posted to a battery here which is only in the embryo stage. This may mean being stuck here for ages. To fill in time, I have applied to go on a refresher course in gunnery at the Imperial School of Instruction, Zeitoun, near Cairo, as I have forgotten a lot of it, and it may give me a better chance of going up the line afterwards.

It is an extraordinary thing, but six other officers from my Brigade in Ireland have followed Davies and me out here—one major (Marshall), two captains and three subalterns. They brought news that no less than fourteen, including some from other Brigades, managed to get their applications through for France. They also said that my messing book had been taken up and published throughout the whole of the Irish Command. The funny thing is there was nothing in it except the obvious. No wonder there are so many army books circulating around to no purpose.

The bathing here is glorious. The other day there was a 2,000 yards swimming race open to the Army and Navy. I went in for it but was nowhere near fast enough. The first three [winners] were in a class by themselves. It was a nasty choppy sea and

143

the last half mile was dead against the wind. The winner was an Australian champion, a West Indian came second and the third, oddly enough, was a sailor.

I have come to know a delightful family here who live quite close to these Barracks—Mr and Mrs Serjeant with three sons and two daughters. Mr Serjeant is Chief Engineer of the Railways out here, and was in the expedition to Khartoum with Kitchener, whom he knew well. He is also a very fine artist. With his large moustache he reminds me of a short edition of Uncle Julian and is always pulling everyone's leg. Mrs Serjeant is French. The eldest son is in England at an O.T.C. camp. The elder daughter, Gabrielle, is a very nice girl of eighteen. She has laughing eyes, she is a fine swimmer and sings beautifully. It was quite breathtaking to hear her sing some lovely French and English songs at a little party at their house. The other two sons, Dean [Dean rose to the rank of Colonel, D.S.O., R.F.A. in the Second World War] and Charlie, aged sixteen and fourteen [respectively], are at school in Alex. and are also fine swimmers. They all speak English, French and Arabic with equal fluency. The other daughter, Bee, is a pretty child of six. It is quite a home for me as they have told me to drop in whenever I like and have offered to keep any kit I may wish to leave. On several occasions, they have taken me to the Sporting Club where we played golf or tennis and, last Saturday, Gabrielle and the two boys came with me for a sail in the harbour. It is lucky that their house is so close and has a telephone because, although I was orderly officer yesterday, I was able to spend most of the day with them instead of twiddling my thumbs in an uncomfortable mess all on my lonesome.

There are several nice fellows in our mess. One is a subaltern called Tower who rowed a good deal at Trinity before the war. [He stroked the Cambridge boat.] We were going to have a go in one of the double scull 'funnies' that could be had from the Rowing Club in the harbour, but he is off up the line tomorrow to rejoin his old Battery.

There is another subaltern, Maitland, who told me of a row

he had with the A.P.M., an officious blighter. One day Maitland was talking to a friend who was standing in a queue for the tram (a sort of road-train that goes through the town) when the A.P.M. came up and, in a nasty voice, ordered him to get in the queue. Maitland replied, 'No, sir,' 'What is this?' barked the A.P.M. 'Do you mean to say you refuse to obey my order?' 'Yes, sir.' The A.P.M. thereupon took his name and particulars and said he would report him to Headquarters. In due course, Maitland was summoned to the office of the Colonel Commandant, who asked him if the report he had received was correct. Maitland said it was, whereupon the Colonel said that that being so, he had no option but to send him to the G.O.C. On arrival at the G.O.C.'s Headquarters, there was the A.P.M. who marched him in like a prisoner before General Boyle. The General told Maitland that he had been brought before him for refusing to obey an order of the A.P.M. to get into the queue that was waiting for a tram, and asked him if that was so. Maitland replied 'Yes, sir.' 'But why did you refuse?' asked the General. 'Because, sir, I did not want to get on the tram.' The General burst out laughing and dismissed the case, much to the rage of the A.P.M.

Talking of General Boyle, two of us subalterns were detailed to support him on the platform one evening in a large hall where a famous Scottish preacher was to give an address to the troops. We were not sure what our duties were to be, but thought we might be required to sit near the General and nudge his elbow if we thought he was dozing off. Anyhow, we found that all we had to do was to sit with several other officers to the right and left of him facing the audience, while the preacher gave his address.

The preacher was a striking looking man with a beard, bushy eyebrows and fierce eyes. He spoke very forcibly in his broad Scotch and waved his arms about. It was quite an arresting talk on the need for meticulous obedience to the very last letter, i.e. no shirking of duty, however trivial. He illustrated this by the story of Naaman, when he was told to bathe in the

Jordan seven times. With a great flourish he said that if Naaman had not obeyed completely, and had failed by one little point such as bathing six times and a 'bittock', he would never have been cured.

Everyone seemed to enjoy the address, judging by the applause at the end.

Another fellow here told us the story of his embarkation at Marseilles some two years before. They had to rig up their 18 pounder guns fore and aft of their ship for defence against submarines. As they had never done any naval gunnery, the O.C. Troops ordered my informant and another subaltern to go aboard a nearby cruiser and get some hints. On mounting the gangway, they found an atmosphere of great agitation because Kitchener was expected any minute. The officer of the watch, or whatever he calls himself, asked them in a voice of extreme exasperation what the hell they wanted. They told him they had been sent to find out how to shoot at submarines. 'Point your damned guns at them and get out!' So they reported back accordingly to the O.C. Troops.

One of the officers who has arrived from Ireland is Captain Macknie, who was Adjutant at Kildare. He is not a bad chap really. We went out to a party at some hotel where he certainly did himself well. We had been laughing a lot and on our way out, when I looked at his bright red face, protruding jaw, gleaming little eyes and his two rows of teeth bared in a grin, I told him he looked just like an inebriated baboon, which, indeed, he did! He became very huffy at this and told me it was a damned cheek for me, a subaltern, to speak like that to him, a Captain. I thought it was stupid of him to flaunt his rank, but as he must be more than twice my age, he had perhaps some grounds for umbrage.

Last Monday on being handed my mess bill I realized with a shock that I could not pay it, having had a bad day at the races on Saturday. After throwing myself into a chair in great despondency wondering whatever I could do about it, I happened to look up and saw on the board an O.H.M.S. letter addressed to me. Mournfully I got up and took down the letter. On opening it, what was my surprise and delight to find it was a notification from the War Office that I had been awarded a wound gratuity of £250. It was indeed a bolt from the blue because I never expected such a thing, but it saved my bacon, full measure and flowing over. The six of us who were marooned in the mess that night had quite a party.

CHAPTER 17

Cairo, etc.

I am at present at the Imperial School of Instruction at Zeitoun, near Cairo.

Shortly after being posted to a Battery some few miles outside Alex., I was sent here for the refresher course in gunnery for which I had applied: it lasts about three weeks. Captain Driscoll is one of the instructors. Stewart, by some lucky chance, is also here on a course of sorts. We found ourselves sitting next each other at lunch one day and on the other side of me was a cavalry subaltern whom A.P. and I used to go hunting with in Ireland. We went to the races yesterday where I met Major Primrose, R.F.C., who was on our ship coming over and who suggested my joining his outfit as they were short of pilots. He introduced me to his Colonel who had been in the 11th with Uncle Julian.

The course is quite enjoyable. We get up at dawn and after two and a half hours' mounted work return simply 'ravishing' for breakfast at which we usually consume porridge, six eggs and four sausages, bread and marmalade, and much coffee. After that is gun drill. There is one officers' squad and an N.C.O.s' squad which drill separately. Some of the fellows in our squad are rather slack, and the instructor on several occasions has had to shout 'Stand still the officers, please', when we are supposed to be at attention. I have never heard him having to pull up the N.C.O.s' squad. The rest of the day is spent in lectures and exams concerned mostly with a lot of impractical nonsense. Knotty problems in geometry and much long division which I loathe. Officers who fail are considered unfit to remain in the Gunners and are sent to the Infantry. One poor fellow, who has been with horses all his time and has broken in 400 and done Captain's work for the last year, is almost bound to fail. I have spent an hour with him every night trying to explain to him the day's lectures. With all these 'tans' and 'cotans' and 'probability factors' and 'solutions of triangles', etc., all mixed up together, it is rather muddling for him.

I think I will pass myself, but that is not due to any knowledge of practical gunnery, but merely because I did a certain amount of that sort of thing at school. Most of the instructors themselves think it rot, but have to kow-tow to the O.C. who was a schoolmaster.

It is three weeks since I returned from the refresher course and on arrival at the Base was told to hold myself in readiness to go up the line. I was bubbling over with the idea of getting there while the advance on Jerusalem was on, and went off to that kind family [the Serjeants] to say goodbye. Then a message arrived from the Colonel to say that there had been a mistake and that I had been reposted to this Battery at Metras and had to report the following day. I nearly wept with rage and disappointment having to potter round here while a moving battle is in full swing in Palestine. However, there have been compensations if only very meagre ones.

There are two Batteries in training out here, each with six guns. The Officers' mess is in a wooden hut. We all live in tents. The O.C. of our Battery is a queer chap who keeps to himself, drinks a good deal and seldom comes on parade. The Captain is a barrister who was in the Sudan Service, and is generally away doing jobs of Judge Advocate and things like that.

We three subalterns are left to run the Battery and do all the training. The senior sub. is a remarkable fellow called Forsdyke [later became Curator of the British Museum and was knighted] who was Curator of the Greek and Roman Department of the British Museum. His company is very stimulating and we have become friends. He is well known among the wealthy Greek community in Alex. who naturally want his opinion on Greek vases and other ornaments which they have in their houses. He has introduced me to quite a number of them, and we have been made honorary members of their swagger Mohamed Ali Club where we sometimes watch them playing cards for enormous stakes. The other subaltern was, at first, old Macknie who, much to his disgust, had to revert to subaltern. He left shortly afterwards to join the Bedfordshire Yeomanry. I was sorry, as he had been very good company in the mess. In his place has come Wesley-Smith, who had been doing his military service with the Argentine Army when war broke out. His father owns a huge ranch out there. He asked the authorities there if he might complete his service with the British Army, and so get some experience of actual combat. This was refused, and it was only after completion of his two years' service with them that he was able to come over and join up. He is a very fine horseman. There is also a very nice fellow named Kydd who is a subaltern in the other Battery.

A Jesuit Chaplain often comes to our mess and cheers us up. He is a rattling good fellow in every way. Being a very learned chap, the conversation between him and Forsdyke runs deep, often too deep for me to follow.

Our camp is some two miles beyond the end of the tramlines where it reverts to desert. A lot of donkey boys hang around there to offer us rides to the camp which, of course, we take. Our Sergeant-Major who is large and fierce-looking, looks very comical, all booted and spurred astride one of these small donkeys, which is being urged to a trot by a little Arab boy running behind with a stick.

Since we have been here, our daily rations have consisted of nothing but rabbits, which have been shipped over from Australia with the troops. We have strict orders to return the skins which are made into jerkins and are on issue to all ranks as may be required. Forsdyke has one; it is certainly very warm.

Stewed rabbit every day could have become rather monotonous had not Forsdyke brought with him from Salonika a haversack full of pearl barley. This, with the aid of sauces, has enabled our cooks to prepare many varieties of savoury dishes.

There has been a lot of thieving in the camp in spite of guards posted all round at night. The Arabs are complete experts at worming their way naked and unseen along the ground. The Major had his uniform trunk stolen from under his camp bed while asleep in his tent. Equipment kept disappearing, to such an extent that it was decided to make a raid on a nearby village. So, one morning, the Battery went off as if on normal exercise and halted near the village. The men dismounted, leaving one man to three horses, and the rest converged on the village and started a systematic search of the mud houses. The women kicked up a tremendous hullabaloo when our men entered their rooms, but a great deal of our missing equipment was found there.

There is a famous restaurant in Alex. much frequented by officers and their lady friends, called Groppi, where one can order ornate cream cakes and iced drinks at reasonable prices. Their iced coffee, served in tall, slender glasses with about three inches of whipped cream on top, is a speciality. It is always so well patronized by the Westminster Dragoons, that they have come to be referred to all over Alex. as 'Groppi's Horse!'

Shortly after my last letter, a wire came ordering me back to the Artillery School as an Instructor. I was very upset about it. Having already refused the job when offered it at the end of the refresher course, to be peremptorily ordered back here by G.H.Q. was a bit thick. Anyhow, I suppose it is a bit of a compliment, and also Driscoll is here, while the other two instructors are exceptionally nice fellows. One of them knew Harold at Cambridge.

It was a blow leaving the Battery. They were a splendid lot of fellows. The sergeants had all seen service on various fronts and were quite first class. There was a very active games committee which organized rugger, soccer, concerts and indoor games under its various sub-committees, with a central fund to which all the Battery subscribed. Forsdyke started it and left the running of it entirely to the men themselves and they did it very well. It took me about an hour saying goodbye. What is more the Battery is likely to be sent up to the line very soon.

On arrival here, I asked to be sent up to the front for a fortnight or so to gain some local knowledge before starting lectures, etc., but they would not hear of it.

My job consists mainly of instructing classes in practical work and also lecturing, chiefly the N.C.O.s, but sometimes the officers. The officers' class includes three captains and a major and they looked a bit surprised to find a young subaltern (who should obviously have been up at the front) lecturing to them. Of course, off parade, I naturally address them as 'Sir'. One morning, when it was my turn to drill the squads, I had the pleasure of shouting 'Stand still the officers, please'.

The place has its compensations. There is the chance of learning a number of things that will be useful at the front. Then there are Wednesday and Saturday afternoons off when we are able to play polo, or rather, a travesty of it, on the main parade ground, which is nearly as hard as concrete. Our mounts are Battery horses which, of course, are quite untrained to the game, but it is good fun and splendid exercise. The great thing here is that it costs practically nothing to live. But nothing will compensate for not being allowed to get up to Palestine, and I asked Driscoll, who is my immediate boss here, if there was any chance of getting away soon. He said he would speak to the Commandant. The latter was very nice about it, I told him I wanted to see some service again before the war was over. He said he quite understood my feelings and told me to put in an application, which he promised to forward, and that he would do his best to get me back to my Battery.

I am back with the Battery, thank goodness, and may be able to see a little fighting in the course of the next month or two.

The other day I received a formal letter signed by General Allenby C. in C., worded thus:

I am glad to congratulate you on being classified 'Distinguished' in the last Officers Artillery Course at the Imperial School of Instructors, Zeitoun.

It is ridiculous! I have never deserved anything less in my life. Merely getting good marks on a course full of geometry exams—also I never did much work on the course. I am surprised General Allenby consents to sign rot like that.

While at Zeitoun I managed to get two days' leave and spent Christmas with that nice family in Alexandria. We went to the theatre on Christmas Eve—some English company. After spending all Christmas Day with them, I caught the train back at 11.30, arriving in Cairo at 6.15, just in time for parade at 6.30.

We came up the line and are now at the Front, such as it is. It is a very dull sector where we gaze at a lot of sand-dunes, and it looks as if we shall be stuck here for the rest of the war.

The journey up was quite interesting. We travelled in a rather primitive train. All the horses were in open trucks. They could not be packed like sardines as the halter rails were on one side only, and the horses were liable to fall when the train jolted. Sentries were posted on the top of the covered trucks, in which the men travelled, to give the alarm if any horses fell. If one did, the train then stopped and we went to the rescue. Sometimes there were several down in one truck with their legs waving about in the air. We then unloosened all their halters. One of us would creep gingerly in, give vigorous kicks to the nearest couple lying on their backs and jump for it. There followed a tremendous scrimmage with legs lambasting the floor and sides and they were all soon on their feet again. When halters were fixed the train moved on again. This performance happened nearly a dozen times, but the horses were none the worse for it, except for a few abrasions.

When we passed some ruins near Gaza, Forsdyke told one of the sergeants of the escapades of the Crusaders there. The sergeant replied that he was most interested to hear about it and must really study his Bible!

With any luck I may get on to something more interesting than sitting here where we hardly fire a shot. Major Greaves, who commanded one of the Batteries whose messing I inspected in Ireland, has written to me that he is to organize a branch of the Intelligence and would like me to join him. He said it might mean going on trips behind the enemy lines with Lawrence. I naturally replied in the affirmative, so we shall see what we shall see.

We have been able to have some pleasant diversions to break the monotony here. We subalterns take it in turns to take charge of the wagon lines, and, when down there, are able to take the horses for a bathe in the sea. The beach where we take them is sandy, with a very gentle slope, so that we can ride them out quite a long way. We ride them naked and, of course, bareback. When the horses start getting out of their depth, they tend to become nervous and want to go back, so we slip off their backs, catch hold of their tail and are pulled to the shore at great speed.

The other day a few of us from the Brigade joined some cavalry blokes in a jackal hunt. There were twelve of us, all armed with revolvers. We did our own beating, through grass as high as the horses' withers. The country was rather broken with small wadis [dry streams] which were often invisible through the grass. When we put up a jackal the fun began. It dodged about and doubled in its tracks with the greatest alacrity, sometimes right under a horse's belly. We could not see it, but could tell where it was by the movement of the grass.

Revolvers blazed away in every direction and, as we galloped through the long grass, some would go head over heels into the wadis. It was quite exciting while it lasted. As you can imagine, we never hit a jackal! Except for a few cuts and bruises, there were no casualties among us huntsmen or our steeds. It was a most enjoyable outing and we hope to foregather again next week.

CHAPTER 18

General Staff Intelligence

On the 1 March orders came for me to report at once to G.S.I. Cairo, and I was given three hours to hand over, pack and get to the station.

On arrival in Cairo, Major Greaves met me and outlined my duties. He gave me authority to procure a motor cycle on return to Palestine and proceed at once to the operations in progress near Jericho. We had two hours together during which he told me that there had been a great tug-of-war over me between the G.O.C., Artillery, General (Long) Smith, and the Head of the General Staff Intelligence, that Smith had been overruled and was very angry. Just then an order came from G.H.Q. Palestine for me to catch the next train, due to leave in four hours, and report immediately on arrival. This I did, but was told on arrival that no one could see me until the following day.

The next day I was told that the orders Major Greaves had given me were cancelled, and that I was to do secretarial work in the Office of a Political Intelligence Captain. He had seen no service and had only been in the Army two years, having been a Cook's agent before that. His first remark to me was, 'Can you type?' My reply, as you can imagine, was an emphatic 'No!' My job was to extract information affecting Economic Intelligence from piles of files of political stuff, and to 'deal with it'. Also to prepare a potted summary of the various Economic Reports for the Daily Diary. After protesting pretty strongly without avail, I set to work. I also prepared a scheme for ensuring what seemed to me a more effective means of procuring information from the various divisions engaged in operations, and which, incidentally, would entail personal visits. This I took yesterday to the G.S.O. (1), Colonel Deedes (who seemed pleased with it) and then asked him to be allowed to go on the job I was originally intended for.

He was surprised to learn that I had been sidetracked and there and then dictated a letter to the Intelligence Heads of the three Army Corps telling them of the opening of a Special Branch of the Economic Intelligence, explaining its purpose and the kind of information required, and adding that he was sending an officer to all Corps, Divisions and Field Units to assist them in this work.

The same day the G.S.O.2, Major Woods, gave me three letters signed on behalf of Colonel Deedes, addressed to the General Staff of the three Corps saying:

This officer has been instructed to visit you and give any assistance that may be required in tracing the economic situation of the enemy from captured material, etc. I should be much obliged if every facility could be given to him.

These I was to take with me.

When I told my Babu Boss that I was off, he seemed annoyed and said that I would lose £50 a year by this because as an officer at G.H.Q., my appointment would be Staff Lieutenant, First Class, but if I went out, my appointment would be Second Class. I told him that that was just too bad. If he thinks I am going to be stuck here as a clerk, he will have to think again.

Unfortunately, the Jericho operation will probably be over before I get away, but something else may soon turn up.

AMMAN RAID

I have just returned from my first little campaign on this front. About three weeks ago, I went to railhead [Ludd] to collect a motor bike and was issued with a $2\frac{1}{2}$ h.p. Douglas which, of course, was quite inadequate for the job, and set off to Jerusalem to report to Corps H.Q. of the Division that was staging a show. They refused to let me go as I had no servant or kit. In answer to a telegram to G.H.Q., a servant arrived who was quite unfit for general service so I had to make arrangements for him to follow me with my kit only as far as Jericho. Then I went on to the Division concerned and reported to the R.A. H.Q., where I explained the nature of my duties. They were most friendly and helpful and advised me about which Brigade to attach myself to. That night I slept in an empty house in Jericho and next morning cycled on to find the Brigade. This meant crossing the Jordan by a bridge called Goroniyeh (the troops had another name for it!) and hunting about, pushing the bike through streams and bushy country. There was quite a bit of firing going on, but, finally, after six hours' hunting, I found the Colonel of the Brigade. He was standing on a rise, watching the effect of his guns through field-glasses. He was most charming, but asked me to stand by for a few minutes as he was rather busy with a battle. He then said how pleased he was to have me with him for the next few days.

Our troops started to advance towards the escarpment. The Colonel asked me if I would go ahead and look out for a suitable camping site. The road wound upwards through a narrow valley with a mountain stream at the bottom. It was not easy going. The road was narrow and edged with boulders, and I had to pass a lot of Infantry on the march. At last I was clear and thankful for an easier spell, hoping soon to catch up the Cavalry which I naturally presumed were ahead. After about two miles, I saw a tent up the hillside about 100 yards off the road with some men in grey coats with rifles slung over their shoulders, whom I took to be Bedouins. I did not take much notice as all my attention was on the road which was very bad. Suddenly, on rounding a bend I saw a German soldier sitting on the side of the road. He lifted his rifle, but lowered it when he saw me slowing down. I stopped to ask him why he had a rifle, thinking he was a prisoner whom the cavalry had told to walk back. After giving him a biscuit I made signs to him to chuck his rifle away. He, thinking, I suppose, that our cavalry had overtaken their rearguard and that he had been left behind, did what I wanted, and then pulled out his automatic which he handed to me and also his dagger, saying, 'Finish war.' My school German just sufficed to ask him if he had seen any *'Englishen soldaten'* and when he answered *'Nien',* I knew what he meant and that I must have gone too far, so I left my motorbike on the side of the road and told him to walk back with me. He looked rather sick at being had for a mug, but as he was disarmed, he had no alternative.

On the way back, two of those 'Bedouins' I had passed came towards us. The German pointed to them saying 'Tourk'. This was a bit of a shock, but when we met they did not take much notice because they took me for a German Officer (I had red tabs and a red and blue G.H.Q. armlet on). Fortunately I had two biscuits left and gave them one each and then pointed to myself saying, 'Me English'. They shook their heads and laughed at first, but the German, who could speak a little Turkish, explained that I really was English. After a bit of palaver they threw their rifles away and preceded us on our way back. Then round the next bend we saw three more Turks with a loaded pony coming up the road. For a moment I wondered what to do. Three alternatives flashed through my mind— to give myself up (horrible thought), to jump on my bike and dash past (pretty hopeless), or to take them prisoner, too. I decided to try the last, so turned about towards my bike saying, 'More biscuit', making the prisoners come with me. There I unloaded the box on the carrier on the plea of getting more biscuits and took out my revolver, as I was not sure how the Bosch one worked. Then we retraced our steps towards the other three. I relied again on being taken for a German and walked casually with the others, keeping my eyes on them all the time, having warned them to keep their mouths shut. I liked the look of the German and, as I had heard there was no love lost between Germans and Turks, decided to trust him. I handed him back his dagger, patting him on the shoulder at the same time. He smiled, and said, 'Tourk, no goot.'

When we reached the other three I tried the same trick but with cigarettes. There were only three left in my case. The first tried to take two, which made me very angry and I shouted at him. He meekly put one back. They looked hungry and slightly dispirited. While they were lighting up, the German went behind and rattled the bullets out of the magazines of their rifles which were slung behind them, saying, 'English goot'. I stepped back and showed them my revolver while the German disarmed them and handed me one of their bayonets which had a saw edge on one side. Then I ordered about turn. The German led with the pony, then the five Turks and then myself with revolver in one hand and the saw-edged bayonet in the other. One tried to grab his rifle, but thought better of it when I shouted at him and he saw my revolver pointing at his head.

And so we marched on, with me hoping against hope that we should meet no more Turks. They shuffled along so slowly that I prodded the rearmost in the back with the bayonet, shouting 'Higgery'. At last, round a bend, was the head of our Infantry who, when they saw our cavalcade, rushed forward shouting, 'Hands up', but I sang out from behind, 'It's all right, they are my prisoners', and handed them over to the O.C. of the Company, who was highly surprised and amused at a G.H.Q. chap being mixed up in this affair.

While I was handing them over the Australian Cavalry passed us, so I hurried back to my cycle, but it was too late. Naturally, thinking it had been left behind by the retreating enemy, they had stripped it of everything including my warm clothes which I was counting on in the absence of my kit. There was nothing for it but to go on until I found a reasonable camping site for the Brigade. It was getting dark when they arrived, and I shared a bivouac with one of the officers which I was glad of as it rained a good deal during the night.

Next morning I set off on my bike, back to Jericho, to find my servant and pick up my kit. The road was terrible. I had already broken both brakes and the pedals, hitting into great boulders and the front tyre had burst, then came the mud almost ankle deep which choked up the machine so that it would not move. After struggling with it for three hours, I had to abandon it on the side of the road and go on on foot, as many other cyclists, even on Triumphs, had had to do. After a ten-mile walk I reached Jericho to find my servant and kit had not turned up. Fortunately I discovered that the R.W.F. were only a mile away so went there and found Morgan [a school friend] who gave me a meal, which was nice, as I had been on the road eleven hours without any food. Two sticks of cordite from a shell case I had picked up, and which looks like macaroni, had come in very useful as straws for drinking from banks of streams. It was dark by then, so Morgan made me share his bivouac for the night. Next morning I set off to find the Brigade. After a four hour trudge through the mud, I ran into the R.A.H.Q., where I was given lunch and a wash—the first for three days. Then I met an officer in the same show as mine, but in another job, who was going up in a car. He gave me a lift. Several times we had to get out and push, but, after about fifteen miles, we reached the old town of Es Salt where I found the Brigade in time for supper.

The Brigade was very kind and gave me blankets, and the Colonel made me share his little tent. It was very cold up there —damp and raw, with rain, sleet and hail. The town was very picturesque, with steep narrow streets, and so were the Arab warriors, armed to the teeth riding their well-caparisoned steeds. The population were tremendously pleased to see us, and to show it some of them brandished their rifles in the air, firing at the same time. All the Bedouins have rifles and love firing them at every opportunity. The General had issued a fulsome proclamation about delivering them from the Turks and invited their co-operation in driving them out of the country. A number of them fell upon a body of Turks with great gusto and put them to flight. The enemy made off as hard as they could to Amman.

Next morning, although the Colonel suggested that I should

rest a day with them, saying I would get no thanks for undue zeal, I thought it best to push on and managed to borrow a mule. After about twelve miles through endless bogs, I came across twenty enemy motor lorries which had got bogged down and been left derelict: in them I found some interesting things from the intelligence point of view. There had been some tribal fighting between two villages near by, and there were a few bodies of men and women lying about. About three miles further on, two armed Bedouins rode up to me and made signs that they wanted ammunition. I had heard that they would cut one's throat for such luxuries as boots, but remembering how when approached by some Pathans with homicidal intent you laughed at them, with happy results, I thought it worth trying this, too. So, slapping each of my pockets in turn, I roared with laughter and shook my head. They were so surprised with this performance that they joined in the laughter. Then, waving my hand, I turned away on my mule and at a leisurely walking pace kept on laughing and shaking my head till I got to the crest of the rise about 200 yards off, expecting any minute to get a bullet in the back. They must have thought me quite mad. As I reached the crest, I heard two rifle shots, but whether that was a farewell salute, I do not know. Anyway, I turned and waved and that was the last I saw of them.

After a further ten or twelve miles I heard some gunfire and went on to find out what was happening, eventually reaching some large rocks where I found two F.O.O.s of the Mountain Artillery. It was Good Friday and we were near Amman. We came under some shell fire which seemed quite strange after so long.

After chatting a bit with them, I went on to the Infantry, who were held up in front of the town which seemed to be strongly defended. As there was little chance of finding anything of interest there, I returned to my mule. By this time it was dark, raining hard and very cold. I got quite lost and after riding round for some hours lay down on a pile of stones, which seemed preferable to the bog, and 'wished for the dawn'. When I got up and was wondering which way to go, a faint whiff of fried bacon reached my nostrils, so I followed my nose and there, round a rise was the Mountain Artillery H.Q., where I was given the most wonderful possible breakfast of bacon and biscuits fried in fat, in front of a roaring fire, and hot tea with rum in it. I gave the Colonel news of his F.O.O.s and returned that day to the Brigade at Es Salt.

On Easter Day, I had set off with the Colonel on his rounds, when orders came that the whole Division was to withdraw to the Jordan. Next day we dropped back into the Jordan valley over 3,000 feet below, where the warmth was delightful after all that bitter cold, but it was a sad trip as we felt the inhabitants had been let down—having encouraged them to help us, we were now deserting them. It was pathetic seeing all those people, who had been so overjoyed at our entry, nearly at their wits end, fleeing in their hundreds from the Turk, thronging the roads all day without food, and carrying what they could take with them. The Colonel gave orders to give all help possible. The guns and limbers were packed with women and children and their bits of baggage, but it was a mere fraction of the great throng streaming down. It was mostly the Christian population who came away. I hope we will do something really handsome for them in part compensation for their terrible suffering. Bad news comes in from the villages, how the Turks are murdering men, women and children in revenge for their having helped us.

I recrossed the Jordan with the Brigade to find that my servant and kit had at last turned up in Jericho, and then went in search of my motor cycle which, of course, was no longer where I had abandoned it. After a five hour hunt, visiting Salvage, Signals, R.E.S.H.Q., and everyone I could think of, without much result, I noticed a signaller riding a Douglas which looked something like mine. A few seconds afterwards, the C.R.A.'s car came by with the Brigade Major who hailed me to give me a lift. I told him that a fellow had just passed me riding my bike, so we gave chase and soon overtook him. As we passed, I scrutinized the bike and spotted a certain small control lever on the left handlebar, the end of which had been broken off on my bike, and so it was on this. We stopped the rider and I asked him where he had got the cycle from. He said he had been handed it by a certain Cable Section to take a message. I told him to take his message and return the bike to the Section. Meanwhile I went to the Section and told the Captain that I had seen one of his men riding my cycle. He looked rather embarrassed, and said he had found the cycle abandoned on the roadside and was going to send it on at once to Corps H.Q., but had lent it to the signaller to take an important message. This was rather disproved on the return of the signaller, as some distinctive markings had been removed. Anyhow I did not wish to kick up a fuss since they had put the bike in working order, with oil and petrol, etc., so off I tootled on it. Next morning I took leave of my kind friends in the Brigade and then saw my Bosch in the prisoners' cage. He gave me a grin and said, 'Goot morgen' (I have written in about his help to me, giving his name, Georg Seigel, and particulars, 703 Regiment, in case he can be given special treatment.)

After calling on the Mountain Artillery, who gave me lunch, I started off for Jerusalem. The bike was a bit of a wreck, but one brake had been mended. All the springs were broken as were the front forks, both pedals, the stand, the exhaust pipe, part of the carburettor and, worst of all, the clutch, and yet it went like the wind. It meant running it along with the engine free, then suddenly putting it into gear and leaping on.

As the Dead Sea seemed only two or three miles off, I decided to have a bathe. It turned out to be seven miles away with heavy going in and out of wadis and took one-and-a-half hours to get there. All around was very desolate and I had a lonesome bathe. The water being a concentrated solution of salt felt very sticky, and I had never realized until then how buoyant it is. One is nearly half out of water. You can't swim breast stroke because your legs just skim the surface. Double overarm is all right. On getting out, some unpleasant hornet like flies attacked me, so I jumped into a pool of fresh water that happened to be near by, which rid me of both the flies and encrustation of salt. There were only some forty-five minutes of daylight left when I regained the road. It would mean spending the night *en route* as my lamp was broken. After about twenty minutes I ran into the Brigade Major in his car again and he made me come along to their mess where I was given an excellent dinner, a shake down for the night and breakfast. It was awfully nice of them as I really have nothing to do with them. The General is a jovial old boy and I enjoyed my stay very much. This morning I reported to Corps H.Q. Apparently the capture of those prisoners must have caused a good deal of amusement since everyone I met seems to know all about it; I heard one fellow say that it was obvious that they should send me across to the enemy with a few more biscuits and cigarettes.

After leaving Corps H.Q., I took my cycle to the H.Q. repair shop in Jerusalem, but they refused to touch it as I belonged to G.H.Q. Since it was too far gone to tackle the mountainous road back, I finally got a lorry to take it and handed it into the M.T. Depôt at Ludd where they tried to make me pay £1 for the missing tools which the Australians had pinched. This I flatly refused to do and told them they were jolly lucky to get the bike back. From there, I came to Jaffa where the H.Q. of the Economic Intelligence has been established. I reported to Major Greaves to whom I submitted a revised plan to increase the supply of information from Field Units, based on the experience of my recent jaunt and also on a tentative itinerary which was to include visits to seven Divisions.

CHAPTER 19

Jaffa

The Economics Section of the General Staff Intelligence operates from three centres, and also has a trade office in Jerusalem.

Here, at Jaffa, are, first, the Old Man (Major Greaves), a gunner of the very old school. He has a very large head, which is bald except for a few white hairs, a prominent hooked nose and small beady eyes. He spent many years in the Civil Administration of the Sudan, where he was known as 'Spitfire Jack'. That cognomen suits him very well, especially when on the telephone, but underneath it he has a very kindly disposition. He has a fund of stories of the Sudan (some taller than others) where he once acted as Civil Secretary. He told us, for instance, that in summer the heat is so great that it is no use to wait for your tea to cool. It merely gets hotter!

Second, is Hough (subaltern), who was Vice Consul in Palestine before the war, a very fine pianist, aged about thirty-five.

Third, comes Sanderson (subaltern), who was a master at Malvern, and is about thirty-five.

Fourth, there is Bennett (Corporal), a master at Rugby, and now Secretary to the Old Man. Aged about thirty (later got his commission).

Fifth, self.

At G.H.Q. Palestine is the 1st Echelon under Captain Graves aged about forty-five, a great expert in Arab and Hebrew literature, and Wilson (subaltern), a master at Winchester, who played cricket for England and is aged about thirty-five.

At G.H.Q. Cairo, is the 2nd Echelon under Captain Ted Dillon, county cricketer and businessman, aged about thirty. A pretty learned lot except for me and, perhaps, Ted Dillon. The whole section, known as G.S.I. (E), and also the Political Section G.S.I. (P), come under Colonel Deedes.

Last month I went to the Remounts Depôt armed with authority to draw two chargers. The Commandant was most helpful and told me I could take my pick from about twenty-five which were walked round a ring for my inspection. I chose a brown gelding that looked as if it could stand up to a lot of rough work and a lovely looking bay mare of about sixteen hands, which had the lines of a race horse. The O.C. told me, after I had picked them, that the mare was known by the name of Loca which means 'mad woman', and was rather temperamental. Anyway she behaved well as I rode her back to Jaffa, leading the other, and she is a most comfortable ride. As the authorities have refused to let me have a groom, Forsdyke, whose battery is in action not far from here, has very kindly arranged to keep them for me whenever necessary. I received a great welcome at the Battery when I took the horses along there. Forsdyke was in charge, with Wesley-Smith and another subaltern. The Sergeants were just the same friendly lot. They were expecting a new O.C. Apparently there had been trouble over the last one who had started to drink more and more heavily. He used to drink on his own and then come out and give some absurd order for Forsdyke to pass on. With considerable risk to himself, Forsdyke used to ignore the orders, if they were too impossible, and give his own instead. This obviously could not go on indefinitely. One day, however, the Major happened to look at the previous day's log from the O.P. and noticed that three Turks had been spotted on a certain ridge. Whereupon, he got very excited saying, 'Let the B . . . . . s have it', and ordered, 'Gun-Fire'. This time Forsdyke passed on the order and there, in this most peaceful sector, was heard a regular bombardment. The Colonel heard it at Brigade H.Q. and naturally wanted to know what the battle was about. So that was the end of the O.C., who was then and there ordered down the line to the relief of them all.

The next day I set off on my new motor bike—a Triumph and a great improvement on the Douglas which is not built for these awful roads—to visit various Divisions in the Eastern Sectors. The road down to Jericho was crowded with long strings of camels. The dust was about six inches deep and covered the lurking boulders. On nearing Jericho, a large boulder knocked my bike over and I lost most of the skin off my kneecap. As I had fallen on the remains of a dead camel, I thought it wise to have it dressed and hunted for a dressing station, eventually finding an Australian one a few miles beyond Jericho. The orderly there swabbed my knee down with neat alcohol, which certainly felt very efficacious, and put on a dressing. That night I stayed in Jericho with a fellow in the Political Intelligence—an interesting chap, who showed me the mounds which were supposed to be the remains of the Jericho after Joshua blew down the walls.

After crossing the Jordan, I came to the bridgehead, composed of barbed wire but with an opening where the road went through. All was peaceful as the Turks had withdrawn to the hills, because the valley was stoking up. After going a mile or so beyond the bridgehead, and seeing nothing of interest, I returned. The heat was terrific—126° in the shade—and so, on coming to a stream, I sat down in it, clothes and all, up to my neck in water, and there chewed an orange. Jumping on my bike afterwards, I returned to Jericho and had a pleasant cool ride while the water evaporated from my clothes; they were quite dry on arrival.

On returning to Jerusalem, I went to see my friends of the Mountain Artillery, who were in the hills north of Jerusalem. The roads were very bad and I had to haul the bike over several stone barriers. In other places one had to use the bike almost like a tank to surmount the obstacles. That night, lying in a bivouac on the Judean mountains (it was pretty cold), I was caught with a spasm of pain in my stomach that made me sweat. It soon passed off, however, but from that day to this I have had a complete stoppage inside me. I probably twisted a gut while struggling with the motor bike.

In Jerusalem, I was held up a whole day for my bike to be repaired and went over to see our Trade Office which the Major had told me to inspect. It was in the charge of a most extraordinary chap we called the Balstoderm. He took umbrage on hearing that I had been sent to inspect his show, and taking off his hat he threw it across the room. By a curious chance, it hit a nail on the wall and stopped there as if on a hat peg, so I congratulated him. He was not amused. In fact, he seemed even more annoyed.

I stayed at the Hardegg's Hotel. The first night, being dead tired, I dropped off to sleep like a log, only to be woken in the early hours with my neck swollen and stinging and smelling a beastly smell. My first introduction to bugs—horrible! I was given a room the next night in another wing, and this was free from bugs. While in Jerusalem, I visited the Church of the Holy Sepulchre, full of all kinds of ornaments and large golden balls, etc. There was a service in progress with several Coptic priests in their black robes, black beards and inverted top hats. They were performing all sorts of evolution. There was an Army chaplain there trying to follow suit, but he was continually being caught out as he did not know what they were going to do next. Just as he had knelt, they were upon their feet, and by the time he had got up, they were facing the opposite way. He, poor chap, looked quite worried over it.

On the morning before leaving, the Military Governor, Colonel Storrs, shared my table for breakfast. He seemed a very polished, brainy chap, and was quite genial.

On returning to Jaffa, after collecting my horses and writing reports, I decided to go to the hospital about my tummy. They took me in for the night and gave me an enema. As it had no affect, they gave me a double one at about 4 a.m. As that had no affect by 8 o'clock, they said they would give me another one, but I demurred and the Doctor ordered me a double dose of castor oil, and said that that would probably do the trick after a good long ride. I was in the saddle most of that day, but still no result! Anyway, it was an enjoyable day and I had lunch with Kydd and Major Paget at their Battery. Much of my time has to be spent these days looking after myself and my horses because of all this red tape about batmen. It does seem stupid.

Much of the front, from the sea and into the Judean hills is situated in sandy country, so I always do my travels in the area on horseback, if possible. The motor cycle just cannot take it except where wire netting has been laid to form roads, the travelling then is quite good; there are, however, many gaps of twenty yards or so, for horse traffic to cross. The only way to span these gaps without getting off and pushing the bike is to put on speed and to hold the front wheel steady while the back wheel swerves around all over the place. It took me some time and many spills to learn this trick. Sometimes the wire netting on these roads gets broken and tends to curl upwards. It catches the bottom of the bike bringing it to a dead stop, and one is shot forward across the handlebars, which can be quite painful!

Ten days ago I thought it would be interesting to go up in one of the two observation balloons that cover the sector to the north of us, so I called on the O.C. of the Balloon Section, saying that I had to report on the state of the crops behind the Turkish lines, and asked if I could have a dekko from one of his balloons. He seemed a little surprised, but then said he would take me along to see a chap called Baker who was due to go aloft in a few minutes. We went by car to the launching place, and there had parachutes strapped on our backs in case the balloon was set on fire by enemy planes. The balloon was attached to a large truck which contained an enormous coil of steel hawser. We climbed into the basket and then started to rise. During the first few hundred feet looking down at the hawser being steadily paid out, I got an awful feeling of vertigo and, clutching the edge of the basket, felt convinced that I could never pluck up courage to jump out and would rather burn with the balloon. However, as we got higher, we got the feeling of being detached from the earth and the spasm completely passed. In fact, it looked as if it would be rather fun to jump out.

The truck to which we were attached then drew us along to the forward area where we had a fine view of the country held by the enemy, from the sea to the hills in the east. When we came down, Baker took me to their mess. The O.C., who was known as the Bimbashi, asked me if I had managed to do what I wanted. On my replying in the affirmative, he said, 'I bet you did because I suppose what you wanted was a trip in the balloon.' I had to admit that this was partly correct. He thereupon invited me to have lunch with them. They seem a cheery, carefree lot of fellows and told me to drop in whenever I am around their way. On leaving, I asked Baker to come to lunch with me in Jaffa on Saturday and go to the races afterwards, where Wesley-Smith was going to ride my mare Loca. He said he could not come as he was on observation duty that afternoon.

Shortly after the races began, we saw a plane making for the balloon and, just after it had passed, the balloon burst into flames. I felt a bit worried and hoped Baker was all right. Just after the third race, Baker suddenly appeared, looking awfully pleased with life, saying, 'Thanks to that Hun plane I have been able to join you after all', and there, in the next race, was my Loca, who came in second—a splendid race—so I was able to introduce Baker to Wesley-Smith, saying he had just dropped from the skies to watch the race.

We have some Gurkha troops in this part of the line who are the terror of the Turks because of their cunning in night sorties. There is also a token force of French and Italian troops, referred to by all as the 'Mixed Vermouth Battalion'. There are also the 'Jordan Highlanders', made up of local Jewish Volunteers. They are still rather raw and not ready to go to the front line; their motto, so rumour has it, is 'No advance without security'.

The other day, Sanderson and I were riding back after a visit to one of the forward Brigades when we saw a company marching towards us on their way up the line. As Sandy is an elderly and rather distinguished-looking chap, I suggested that he should ride in front—the two stars on his shoulder flaps would not be seen and with our G.H.Q. insignia, and me riding behind as his A.D.C., he would be mistaken for a Staff Colonel at the very least. He fell in with the idea. As we approached we heard the company being ordered to march at attention and then received 'eyes right' with a flourishing salute from the O.C., which Sandy graciously acknowledged.

PART SIX

Final Fling
July 1918 to the end

CHAPTER 20

Here and There

I have just returned from an interesting trip to the forward areas north of Jerusalem where I picked up a pair of Uhlan boots that fit me splendidly. They are top boots of the softest black leather and are most comfortable. On visiting the R.W.F., I looked up my friend Morgan who told me his company was going to attack a hill that night which was held by the Turks, so I thought it would be a good thing to join him as there might be some interesting things to be picked up. He took me along to the Colonel who readily consented. As evening approached, Morgan had what he called his 'scuppering parties' assembled, and gave them their orders, impressing on them the importance of silence when eliminating the enemy listening posts. They were picked men who had had special practice in this kind of thing. We moved off just after nightfall. It was by no means pitch dark, as there was a hazy moon in the sky, and we could distinctly see the top of the hill we were to take; it seemed that the Turks would be bound to see us as we moved slowly up towards them. However, everything went off perfectly. The scuppering parties did their job without a sound being heard, and we got within thirty yards before the Turks realized anything was wrong. Then they let fly—a sudden spatter of rifle fire —within less than a minute all was over and we had taken the trenches. I took some samples of their sandbags which interested me because, instead of fibre, they were made of what appeared to be string composed of tightly rolled brown paper. The whole show was over in less than three hours. There were hardly any casualties and only about a dozen prisoners were taken, as most of the Turks were too quick for us and had bolted before we reached their trenches.

The Major was in Jerusalem and, on my arrival there, he took me round to the Arab Bureau where I met some extraordinarily interesting and romantic characters. I wish I were free to be more explicit. The Major also introduced me to a fellow called Weisman who is evidently a big pot in the Zionist world.

At the hotel, I ran across a gunner friend of mine who had been in the advance of Jerusalem. He told me that he managed to get a good view, from the top of a wall, of the investiture ceremonies when the Duke of Connaught came out. There was Allenby, with five or six other Generals, lined up to receive decorations from the Duke. Suddenly the Duke, looking fierce, marched up to Allenby and tapped him sharply on the shoulder. Apparently Allenby had committed the awful crime of appearing on parade with the button of one of his shoulder flaps undone. Allenby smartly took two paces forward, did up the button and fell in again, whereupon the investiture took place.

On my return, I dropped into G.H.Q. for tea and there, at the table, was Lawrence dressed up as an Arab. He looked much younger than I expected, and seemed rather shy and reserved. He may have been feeling off colour.

Jaffa is an unhealthy place during the summer. All of us have been having continual goes at fever. Sand flies are the worst pest. They are so small that they can get through the mosquito nets, and give one a fever that seems more debilitating than malaria. This, and the stagnant heat, makes everyone feel depressed. Some of us were saying how we wished we were back in France as it would be better to be blotted out quickly by a shell than to die slowly of disease out here. 'Oh Palestine the Holy Land, with bugs and fleas, disease and sand.'

Fortunately for me, I happen to be sharing a house with a doctor named Wilson. He also has a motor bike, but is one up on me because it sports a sidecar. He has been dosing me with bottles and bottles of liquid paraffin, but so far to no purpose. He tried to cheer me up by saying that people can go on for months in the state I am in. It does not cheer me much, because it is no fun feeling below par all the time, and my tummy looks like a balloon. In fact, when bathing, my friends make facetious remarks about it!

I forget whether I told you that at last I have managed to borrow a groom who also does batman (he used to be batman to Hough)—an extraordinary fellow. He is quite remarkable in the way he is able to scrounge extra food for my horses and extra bits of harness. He may yet bring trouble on both of us in spite of my admonitions to be more careful. One of my horses got worms rather badly, whereupon Jock told me that in Glasgow they used to cure their dray horses of worms by giving them tobacco, so we got an ounce of tobacco and having covered it with grease shoved it down its throat. It had great effect and the horse seems completely cured now.

I have found, when travelling round the country, that these Jaffa oranges can carry one on for a whole day. On these journeys I seldom know when or where I shall get the next meal as I have to rely on the hospitality of the units I visit. Only once, so far, have I been for more than twenty-four hours without a meal and that was due to my motor cycle breaking down. One of the results of this uncertainty is that I make the most of the hospitality at each place I happen to stop, and then find myself invited to another meal only a few hours later. The result is a constant state of overfedness.

The artillery units everywhere treat me almost as if I were the Prodigal Son and, perhaps, in a way, I am! All the infantry brigades and Divisional people have been most kind and helpful also.

I have been like a blue-bottle since mid-August, dashing about visiting no less than eight Divisions. All the ones in the hills had to be done on motor cycle. It has been pretty hard-going, but with plenty of pleasant diversions. When visiting the 54th,

I had tea with Major Paget and Kydd and afterwards watched the polo. I played in one chukker, but was pretty feeble. Paget was a treat to watch.

On visiting G.H.Q., Colonel Deedes called me in. He told me he had put my name forward for promotion, but it had been turned down flat. Apparently General Smith, the M.G. Artillery, saw it, and wrote, 'I hope Colonel Deedes will not fling this officer back to me as a Captain'. The Colonel told me of the row over my secondment, and he had no doubt that this curt refusal of his recommendation was due to my having got a 'Distinguished' at the artillery course only a month or so before my transfer. He said that he could probably get me my promotion if I cared to transfer from the R.F.A. to the general list of officers. I thanked him, but said I should not like to sever my connection with the Regiment. He said he quite understood my feelings on the matter. Major Greaves was wild about it and is thinking hard how he can help me, but I don't see how anything can be done.

I was laid low for two days with a curious attack of something which left me very weak and shaky, but fortunately it passed sufficiently to let me get going on my tour—Jerusalem, Bethlehem, to mounted divisions and others, often finding that they had moved. The roads were pretty awful and my bike has had to have the rear wheel replaced twice, among other repairs.

As I may be called upon soon to take on some political work, I have had orders to work under what is known as 'Advantel West' [Advanced Intelligence West]. The job has possibilities of being quite interesting. A priceless letter has come from the A.A.G. to G.S.I. headed 'Subject—Officer's Batman and Groom':

Ref. your letter permission is granted for the provision of soldier batman to the officer named and groom in the case of his joining a Mounted Division. These servants should be obtained from the unit to which the officer is attached.

Since I expect to be attached to different units from day to day, what fun we should have! Anyway, it does not matter now because I have Jock as my all-purpose batman and partner in crime.

While in Jerusalem I went to the Arab Bureau and there met a most jovial Friar just starting off on his mule into the blue with a bag of gold. He threw it in the air once or twice and then with a chuckle hid it under his cassock. Of course, he may not be a Friar.

CHAPTER 21

Nazareth

Here I am in the Dysentery ward of Ras-el-Tin Hospital at the far end of Alexandria Harbour, after nearly a month in Nazareth. Now that the war is over as far as we are concerned, I am quite pleased to be here where one can just lie doggo and sleep—the only ordeal being the 6 a.m. wash.

Nazareth is a picturesque town, most of the streets being on steep slopes, and there are some fine views from the hills around it. The population consisted of two to three thousand Moslems and seven to eight thousand Christians, but no Jews. It was a bad place for fever, with all manner of vermin that interfered with sleep at night. The water was undrinkable as the wells were nearly empty and people were dying of malaria and dysentery. Fortunately for me, I found a lot of German wine, rather like champagne. This, together with tins of bully which the Australians kindly left me, and the few eggs I was able to buy, made up my daily diet for most of the time I was there.

As I had no money with me, I bought the eggs with some Austrian hundred krone notes that I happened to find there. The natives rather grudgingly sold me two eggs for one of these notes—but I must start at the beginning.

I had arranged, just before the show began, to join the Essex Battery, but as it was evident that urgency for samples would end if the advance went well, I was switched to the general branch and came under Advantel W. and had to make my way forward as best I could. Everything went wrong to start with. I had sent Jock forward to railhead with my horses and followed later on my motor cycle, only to find they were not there. A whole day was spent looking for them, only to learn that they were back in Jaffa, with Jock ill in hospital. This meant returning to Jaffa. It was quite maddening with the attack well on its way and with 5,000 prisoners and 70 guns already captured. I took my mare only, leaving Budger with Doc. Wilson, who said he would send him on to me with his batman, George, if I would help George to get to his home in Haifa.

It was dusk before I reached railhead and then rode on towards the Balloon Section at Kalkillie about twelve miles away. Finding my way across country was not easy because clouds hid the stars so I only had the moon to guide me (which, of course, kept moving). However, I was lucky and came up on them about 9.30, where I off-saddled and had drinks with the Balloonists and set off again at 11, arriving at Tulkaram at 2 a.m.; there I fed the mare and dossed down in a field beside her. On waking up next morning, I felt rather groggy, but pushed on to find Corp. H.Q., where Colonel Deedes had just arrived by car with General Buckley, the B.G. 'I'. They told me to concentrate on information about food and forage supplies.

After getting something to eat there, I rode on to Nablus where there were a lot of horses and transport vehicles lying about as the result of a scrap. That night I slept in the open again, setting off next morning, and for the next twenty-five miles there was nothing to be seen—no signs of fighting, no troops, or natives—not even a donkey or sheep.

On reaching Tel Elfule about 4 p.m., I bumped into an Australian squadron and was most hospitably entertained to tea and eggs. We all sat on the ground. The orderlies brought a large bowl full of boiled eggs. We tucked into these while the orderlies stood around joining in the conversation. As soon as an officer had had his fill he got up and an orderly at once plumped down in his place and started eating.

When the meal was over, the O.C. held a pow-wow with his officers and the Sergeant-Major. They were going up to Nazareth that evening, and he was arranging for his various troops to guard it. He told one of the officers to take his troop to the hills on the far side, whereupon he replied, 'Well, I'm not going'. The O.C. looked surprised and then told him that he should be ashamed of himself for talking like that in front of their guest —that was me! However, the troops leader said that 'it was not fair on his 'orses as his 'orses had been 'arder worked than those of any troops that day'. The Sergeant-Major chipped in to say that that was a fact, so after a bit more talk all was amicably settled.

There was evidence of some sharp fighting and any amount of abandoned stores and vehicles on the roadside. The road wound steadily up into the hills and, nearing Nazareth, one had a glorious view of the plain of Esdraelon. I reached Nazareth at dusk and, after having a few drinks with the Australians with whom I had arranged to feed next day, lay down on a sofa in the house of the late Turkish C. in C., Liman von Sanders. After being bitten to bits by mosquitoes, I got up and found a tablecloth which gave me some protection. Liman von Sanders had managed to escape by the skin of his teeth two days before, when the van of our cavalry entered the town, by jumping in a car and driving out the other side. The house was a double-storeyed one, and there was a thunder box upstairs with a shaft leading right down through the house and its foundations, to a deep pit. Judging by the reverberations, it certainly lived up to its name.

The happenings during the next three weeks are rather hazy. They were certainly the hardest and would have been the most interesting I have ever spent had it not been for the fever which made me as weak as a kitten, and for lack of sleep at night due to bugs and mosquitoes. (The best nights I usually had were when I lay on the stone floor.)

On the first day, 24 September, I had breakfast with the Australians, and took over an office in the German G.H.Q. where I met Brunton, also of the Intelligence, on his way to Haifa. He told me that I had been appointed Political Intelligence Officer, Nazareth.

On returning to the Australians, I found they were about to move on for the north. Their doctor saw that I was pretty groggy, so gave me some aspirin, told me to lie quiet, and left me some whisky to take later on. They also left me a quantity of bully to keep me going. They were perfect bricks, ready to do anything for one.

My work consisted of finding out the food position and dealing with it, searching out and examining enemy documents, of which there were tons: I.B. work, i.e. black lists, etc., P.I. work (on political matters); interviewing agents; and generally sorting out the personal problems of hundreds of refugees and other lost souls. I was lucky to find a splendid young Syrian who had been educated at a mission school to act as my interpreter, and eventually got the co-operation of the Mukhters 'headmen' whom I called in several times for their advice. Often I was in my office from 5 a.m. till midnight, sometimes till 2 a.m. The work also entailed a good deal of foot-slogging round the town, but the ever-present fever was a continual drawback.

After the Cavalry left, there was a hiatus of several days before the Infantry arrived and communications opened up. During this time, I was the only Britisher there, without even a batman, and learned later to what profitable use this was put by certain influential scoundrels to feather their own nests and threaten the people against helping us.

Two days after my arrival, I went up to the German Hospice at the top of the hill overlooking Nazareth, as I heard there were documents hidden there, and found the place was being looted right and left. There were crowds of sick folk lying all over the floors on old sacks, etc., and all they had to eat were army biscuits which the Cavalry had left for them. I was lucky to find in the town the man who had been in charge of the grain stores. He was a Syrian Arab and an officer in the Turkish Army. With him, I went round all the stores taking stock and marking them up. As he seemed to be a decent sort of fellow, I gave him the job of arranging for the grinding of the grain, making the bread and carting it each morning to the hospital, for which I let him have 15 per cent of the flour. The arrangement nearly fell through when some blighter accused him of stealing his money. This meant suspending him while I went into his case and had his house searched. As there was no proof against him, I reinstated him and he did a really splendid job of work. When things became more organized, I was able to arrange for his return to his home in Beirut. Before leaving, he unpinned from his breast a Turkish medal, which he handed to me as a memento.

I should mention that to start with I had to rely for help on the Arab gendarmes who had been employed by the Turks, and told them that if they worked well I would recommend them for employment under the British.

During the first few days, I was finding it difficult to get much information on the political situation or news of wanted men, etc., until one night a fellow came to me and told me that the Mayor and the Kadhi, and a number of other leading persons who were all related, were telling the people that the British would be driven out just as they had been at El Salt six months before, and that if anyone helped me with information they would be handed over to the Turks to be hanged. I had previously had several visits from the Mayor about the purchase of corn and livestock for the Army. He was a large oily brute who assured me of his anxiety to help the British in every way. I could see by the way he looked at me that he thought me a complete simpleton. The next day I sent him a message saying that I should be grateful if he and the Kadhi and the other councillors would honour me with a call to discuss some matters of importance. I then told my interpreter to warn six of the gendarmes to be on hand. The Mayor and company arrived next morning and, when they were seated, I called in the gendarmes and told them to march them all down to the prison and lock them up. When the Mukhtars came for a pow-wow that afternoon, I asked them what the reaction was in the town. Their spokesman said, 'The people feel that at last the British have taken Nazareth.' After that, information came pouring in.

People were vying with each other to tell their stories, many of them, of course, being complete lies in order to pay off old scores.

When writing my report on the arrests, I simply could not, for the life of me, think how to spell 'Mayor'! I could only think of my mare, and finally compromised by writing 'Maire' hoping that that might be the French for it.

The stories that came in about the Mayor and his gang were pretty bad. Apart from threatening the people in general against the British, the Mayor had a down on some leading Christians and had sent in the names of twenty-five of them to the Turkish authorities accusing them of spying for the British, and suggesting that they should be hanged. This would have been done had not a decent Turkish Officer of great influence quashed the case. The Mayor also had a huge nigger, whom he kept in outlying villages, to go round at night to rob and beat anyone who had incurred the Mayor's displeasure, and to break up his house. Then there was the story of how the Mayor, when asked to bring in all the Turkish horses and livestock that had been taken by the people, went round ordering everyone to hand over the animals in the name of the Government. Of these, he kept two-thirds for himself and sent them off to his own lands in outlying districts. One lot were said to have been sent to a place of his near Tiberias. I sent a wire to the I.O. who found sixty government sheep there. The night after the arrest it occurred to me that as my bedroom was in an empty house and unguarded, some of the Mayor's pals might try to do me in, so I left the German camp-bed (the first bug-free bed I had found) with the mosquito net down so as to make it look as if I were there, and lay with my revolver behind the door which had no lock, waiting for a visit, but no one came.

Weak as I was, and working all day, I could not manage another night like this, so I wired up the door and lay down on the bed with my revolver under the pillow. I was awakened by a slight noise at the door and, on reaching for my revolver, my bed creaked and I heard a patter of feet. Someone told me afterwards that on such occasions one should always sleep with one's revolver between one's knees.

Out of the flood of information that began to flow in, came a story about the German Bank Manager, how he had gone round the country with an influential Turk—Talaat Pasha, I think it was—trying to stir up the Moslems to slaughter the Christians. As there were other shady stories about him, I felt he should be put inside. He seemed quite an inoffensive sort of chap, so I tried to put him at his ease when asking for his personal details to enter on the form, but he was actually trembling.

A day or two later a Captain turned up at the Turkish Head-quarters and introduced himself as 'Military *Governaar*'. On the following day, he called me in to tell me that he had had a deputation from leading citizens saying that the Bank Manager was held in high esteem and they were upset over his arrest. He proposed to release him, but when I demurred, he said he felt he must override me. I thereupon went to my office and wrote him a letter saying I had, on information received, locked up Mr X and looked to him as Military Governor to see that he was kept in safe custody, ending with the words 'Copy to G.H.Q.'. This letter I handed to him, and, on reading it, he agreed to hold over the release. The result was a telegram from G.H.Q. instructing me to send Mr X down to them under guard imme-diately; so I suppose they must have had something on him, although his name was not on my black list.

After about a week, a very nice fellow, called Suter, arrived in charge of the Guides and Interpreters, so I joined up with him and he kindly undertook to look after my horses. One of his men discovered the whereabouts of a notorious Turkish Officer called Ramsey Bey. His was one of the names on my black list, so we went off in Suter's truck to catch him, but found he had fled. We learnt to our great annoyance that a report about him had been sent the day before to the I.O. of the next district, who had sent a posse after him which had naturally frightened him away. We came back with his shepherd, from whom we learnt where the Bey's wife was, and arranged for a watch to be kept on the house. Later, we heard that the Bey was at a certain village, so went off at once hoping to catch him, only to learn that he had gone to Tiberias. The only thing left to do was to send a wire to the I.O. there.

Dear old Suter went down with a sharp attack of fever with temperature running up to 105°. I acted as nurse. He kept chatting away, saying the most absurd and amusing things in his delirium. However, in spite of my ministrations, he suddenly recovered after two or three days.

A day or two later, General Buckley came up with Major Woods, the G.S.O. 2, to have a look around. He told me that as the advance had got as far as Aleppo, I should concentrate on documents and he would send me some help on this job. I showed them round and, as they seemed to be out for souvenirs, I gave them the German and Turkish flags. While routing through documents, I found a few little mementos such as some German and Turkish medals and epaulettes and also a certificate of award of the Iron Cross, Class II, for Unteroffizer Greenig Bock, signed by Liman von Sanders. I must tell the German authorities about this after the war so that the poor chap gets his medal. Wilson and Seymour Jones, plus two others, arrived to help with the documents. It was very nice having them. They stayed about a week and, after sorting out and packing off everything they thought of value, they left.

Shortly afterwards I called round on a Battalion which had recently arrived at Nazareth on their way north, and was camped in a field just below a deserted hotel. The officers were a delightful crowd and gave me an open invitation to join their mess, which was lucky for me because I was on my last tin of bully left me by the Australians. It was at this hotel that I found the German wine which had kept me going. The following day I happened to go into an inner cellar leading off from the main one to see what might be there, and by a great stroke of luck came across a box full of Major von Papen's personal papers— he was away on leave in Constantinople. There were all sorts of letters and photographs and a plaque of his medal ribbons there, also a number of documents. As some of the documents looked important I hurriedly went through the box and had it locked, sealed and dispatched to G.H.Q., but kept a few mementos, such as his medal ribbons, and a number of his personal photographs, including some snapshots of the Kaiser at the Front in Europe when von Papen was on his staff there, and of General Falkenhein's visit to Palestine; also a personal letter from Count Bernstorff in Constantinople dated 21 October 1917, hoping to visit him (von Papen) in Jerusalem about Christmas time. (Allenby had taken Jerusalem by then.) Among the papers found in this box were details of a plot to stir up a rebellion in India. I sent this down—and was later told that it was published in the local 'comic cuts' to amuse the troops.

Later that day I was asked to accompany an I.O. to Damascus in his box car, which was full of gold, weighing several hundredweight. Unfortunately, the car broke down on the way, and we had an awful job getting it back to Nazareth. It took us most of the night and half the morning. I was feeling pretty rotten by then and had to lie up. The doctor came round and found my temperature was 103°. He took me to the Hospice, where I stayed until fit enough to travel, and then came down here in an R.A.F. tender as far as railhead and then by train. Just after I crocked, I received a letter from Major Woods at G.H.Q. which read:

The B.G. 'I' has instructed me to order you to look after yourself. We cannot afford to have officers through neglect breaking down and catching fevers, etc. You should, if possible, requisition a house on the top of the hill or arrange to live with the military governor. You must be careful with your food and see that you don't eat messy things. I am making arrangements to supply you with a groom, funds and an extra interpreter. Don't overdo it. You have done excellently. Is there anything else you want from here?

When I read it, I did not know whether to laugh or cry. 'Be careful of my food', 'Get a house on the top of the hill'. Why not 'Be sure you have clean sheets every night', and, as for the groom, Suter had taken my horses along with him as I could not look after them. I shall probably never see them again.

There was so much else that happened in Nazareth. All the interviews for hours on end with all sorts of kinds of people—Arabs, Turks, Germans. Information about munition factories, the state of crops in the north, rows between different factions, etc., etc. It all remains a kaleidoscopic dream.

By the way, I have asked one of the sisters to send you a fur hat which I found in Liman von Sanders' bedroom. It is the kind worn by the biggest pots in the Turko-German Army. I hope it will reach you in time to be of use against the rigours of the Kashmir winter.

CHAPTER 22

Ras-el-Tin Hospital

It has been very pleasant here in hospital. Kydd turned up two days after me. I was delighted to see his cheery face again. We have been doing most things together since we were allowed up. There are twenty-four of us in the ward. In the next bed to mine is a cheery red-haired doctor named Hill. One evening, about a week after I came, a newcomer was carried in on a stretcher. He looked like a skeleton as he was being put into a bed opposite mine, with hollow cheeks as white as parchment, and sunken eyes. Then I suddenly recognized him as a friend of mine named Grosvenor. (We heard later that he had caught dysentery somewhere north of Damascus and had travelled in the bottom of a lorry for several days.) He went straight off to sleep as soon as his head touched the pillow. Sometime after midnight a sister came and started shaking him to wake him up. He asked her in a plaintive voice, 'Why, oh why, did you wake me?' She replied, 'I want to give you this pill.' Then we heard him expostulate, saying 'Good Heavens! Just to take a tiny pill like that. I would not have minded so much if it had been a big one!' He looked so quaint when he said it.

Everyone is put on a course of emetine injections for the first sixteen days—one in each arm alternately. The arms get so sore that we have to lie on our backs or our stomachs. The only nourishment has been albumen water. However, to celebrate the Armistice on the 11th, we were allowed to, as a special treat, have a glass of milk and water!

As you can imagine, everyone in the ward had pretty runny

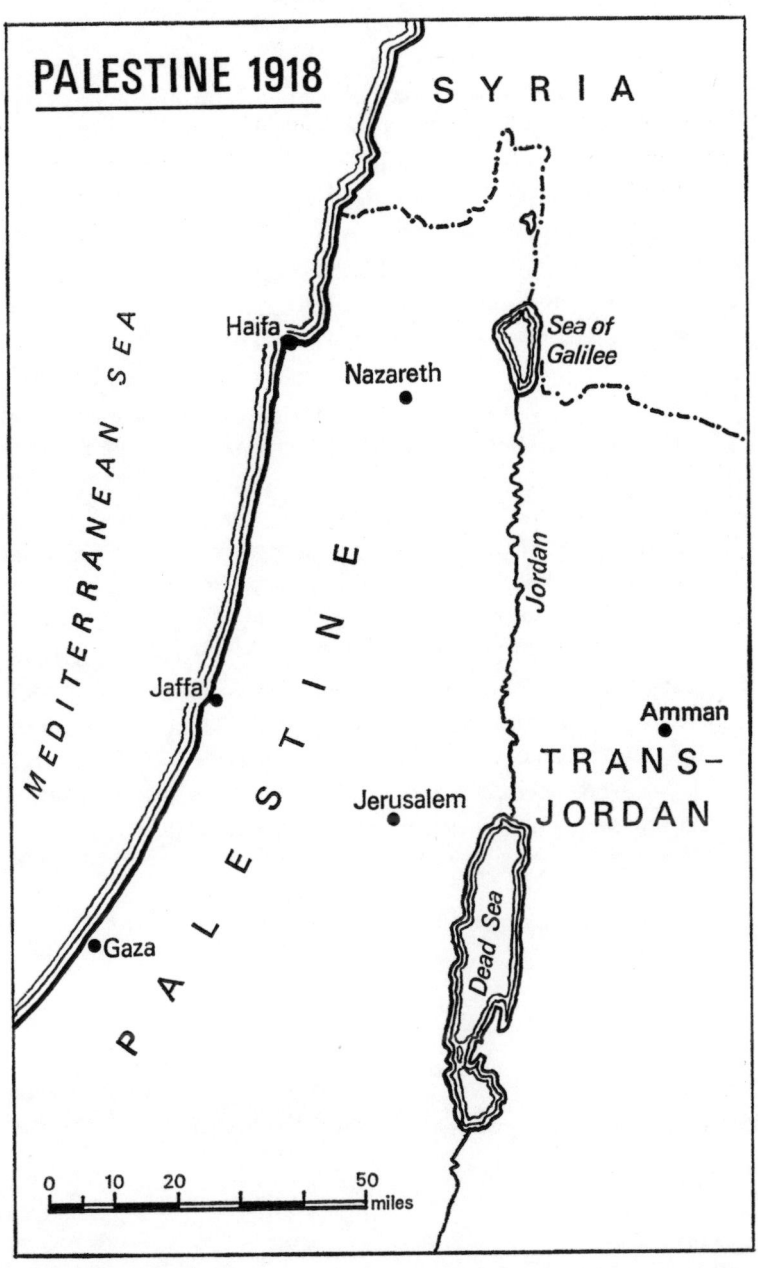

PALESTINE 1918

S Y R I A

MEDITERRANEAN SEA

Haifa

Nazareth

Sea of
Galilee

Jordan

Jaffa

Amman

T R A N S -
J O R D A N

Jerusalem

Dead Sea

P A L E S T I N E

Gaza

0   10   20   50
                            miles

tummies at first. Everyone, that is, except me. It was a matter of lively interest to see how many times those on each side had to take up strategic positions each day. Our side always lost because I was a non-starter! This went on for nearly a fortnight until one morning the great moment arrived when I received the call to play my part. This aroused such excitement that everyone sitting up in bed beat time to my measured tread down the ward and gave me quite an ovation on my return.

Kydd took a snapshot of me dressed up in a red hospital dressing gown, adorned with Major von Papen's ribbons and with the epaulettes and German and Turkish medals I had collected in Nazareth. My hat was on back to front and I held a fly flap up in one hand. The result was more like some Chinese mandarin.

I had a letter from Captain Graves, who is now a Major, saying that Col. Deedes is off to Constantinople with the rank of Brigadier General. He (Graves) is off to Beirut. Wilson is at Aleppo. Sanderson is in hospital at Cairo. About me he writes:

'You are now on the establishment of the G.S.I. as a Second Class Agent, which gives you pay and allowances of a Staff Lieut. 1st Class, i.e. about £30 more than the pay of a Captain in the field. General Buckley was very pleased with your work at Nazareth so that there should be no difficulty in finding employment for you in Intelligence if you wish it.